A PRENTICE HALL GUIDE

Anthropology

ON THE INTERNET

Evaluating Online Resources

M. Neil Browne • Stuart M. Keeley

Bowling Green State University

Chapter 12 by
James G. Duvall III

Prentice
Hall

Upper Saddle River, NJ 07458

©2001 by Prentice-Hall, Inc.
PEARSON EDUCATION
Upper Saddle River, NJ 07458

ISBN 0-13-088825-7
Printed in the United States of America

Contents

Preface

Students increasingly rely on the Internet as their preferred resource for finding information and arguments. We wrote this book largely because our own students have persuaded us that this tendency is part of a long run trend. As the authors of *Asking the Right Questions: A Guide to Critical Thinking*, we have already addressed in a fairly thorough fashion how the art of critical thinking can be applied to books, articles, speeches, and lectures. But we wanted to address a different audience who needs a slightly different set of critical questions when assessing what they think they have learned from websites.

Critical thinking is a set of skills and attitudes for *evaluating* arguments. The arguments made on websites need especially careful evaluation. The ease of access to the Web applies to those who wish to express themselves on the Web, as well as to those who wish to learn from it. Hence, we must use what we find on the Internet with great caution. In this book we describe a process for doing so.

It is unlikely that you are reading this manual without some basic understanding of the Internet and its features. Furthermore, we're pretty confident that most of you have considerable knowledge of the Internet. Numerous "Internet guides" are available to help the beginner connect to and browse the Internet. We recognize, however, that some readers may be new to the Web, so we begin with two chapters on the basics of the Internet. Three appendices provide additional information on documenting online sources, a guide to the Companion Websites which are likely to accompany your Prentice Hall textbook, and a glossary of terms to help you navigate through the terminology you will encounter when exploring the Internet.

The primary purpose of this book, however, is to help you develop a critical-thinking approach to your use of the Internet. After reading this guide you will have the tools to evaluate all the material you find on the Web.

In the preparation of this book, we have been assisted by two talented and creative assistants, Carrie Williamson and Elizabeth Barre. Both are much more than student assistants. Their devotion to high-quality work is inspirational to us as teachers.

For use of material from their Web pages, the authors of:

http://www.netspace.org/herald/issues/100397/speech.f.html
http://www.ceousa.org/
http://www.fcc.state.fl.us/fcc/state.fl.us.fcc/reports/methods/
estamates.html#probs/
http://www.fairtest.org/facts/satfact.htm
http://sun.soci.niu.edu/~critcrim/guns/gun.viol
http://www.calvin.edu.edu/academic/engl/346/proj/vduyn/index.htm

along with BSM Consulting, owners of the copyrighted material at

http://www.personalitypage.com

and Colin Kenny, the author of

http://sen.parl.gc.ca/ckenny/itstime.htm

have all granted us permission.

Chapter 1

Finding Your Way

This thing that we now call the Internet has been evolving ever since it was first developed almost thirty years ago. Its prominence in our society has been increasing exponentially in recent years.

The Internet was born as the solution to a problem. It was designed to provide a global communication channel for the exchange of scientific information and research. Gradually, however, the Internet has also become a digital post office, a digital bulletin board, a digital telephone, and a digital tutor. Its real merit to you is how it will solve *your* problems and make *your* day just a bit more manageable. Hopefully, that is what you'll discover here.

Getting Started

The following URL's are a few of the many beginner's guides available on the Internet. You'll find everything you need to know about modems, browsers, e-mail, bulletin boards, chat rooms, and getting connected to the Internet on at least one of these sites.

An Introduction to the Internet from Interactive Connections

http://icactive.com/guide/index.htm

This is a very comprehensive guide to the Internet. It is provided by Interactive Connections, an Internet Presence Provider. If you need a refresher course on Internet basics or are starting from scratch, then this site will help.

Learn the Net

http://www.learnthenet.com/english/index.html

Learn the Net specializes in online training products and services for the corporate world. Their guide is well written and up-to-date. It is an excellent source of information for the beginner.

Net Guide from PC User Magazine

http://www.pcuser.com.au/netguide/

This guide is sponsored by the Australian version of *PC User* magazine. In addition to a selection of articles about tools and techniques for experienced Web surfers, this site contains many useful resources for the beginner.

Many of you reading this guide have a lot of experience with computers, while others have little or none. Before proceeding, you should have and be familiar with a few basic resources:

1. computers
2. Web browsers
3. Internet connections

Don't worry if you can't afford your own resources. There are many free or inexpensive options available to you, and we'll do our best to show them to you. The use of computer labs is now a common and even required component of most courses. Also, we're pretty confident that these computers have one of the popular browsers by Netscape or Microsoft and an Internet connection. If you haven't found your campus computer lab yet, then our guess is that you'll find it associated with your campus library. From a beginner's point of view, the only real concern you'll have is learning the basics.

Searching the World

Although many wire-heads consider the Internet to be the largest library on the planet, it doesn't necessarily have the easiest card catalog in the world. In this section, we'll explore techniques for searching the Internet, discuss practices for evaluating the validity of the content you find, discuss online education, explain CD-based Companion Website learning, and review guidelines for citing information within your class assignments. With practice, these skills will help you improve your usage of the Internet.

There is one skill, or rather behavior, that you must adopt in order to maximize your time-to-gain ratio. That is, be aware of "search drift." The Internet is an information jungle and if you wander into it without having a sound idea of why you are there, or if you just wander around without being aware of where you are, then you will get "lost" and waste a great deal of time. Yes, there are times when you will want to play, wander, and have a good time, but consider whether the best time to do that is the night before a test.

Searching

Yahoo! is a good place to begin. It is only one of many resources available on the Internet. It's easy to remember. If you have a chance, log onto the site and follow along as we describe how to use it.

Yahoo!: http://www.yahoo.com

2

Yahoo! began as a simple listing of information by category—kind of like a card catalog. As it's grown, it has added the ability to search for specific information—and many, many other features that we encourage you to explore. At the top level of the directory there are several very general categories, but as you move deeper into the directory, notice that the categories become more specific. To find information, you simply choose the most appropriate category at the top level and continue through each successive level until you find what you're looking for (or until you realize you're in the wrong place). Don't be afraid to experiment—it's easy to get lost but also easy to find your way home. Because Yahoo! cross-references among the categories, you'll find that several related categories will lead you to your desired page.

Prepare yourself for a search *before* you jump into one. In the long run, it will save you both time and frustration. Don't be afraid to try some strange approaches for your search strategy. A good technique is to pull out your thesaurus and look up other names for the word. You might be able to find a more common form of the word. Think of everything associated with your question and give each of these subjects a try. You never know what might turn up a gold mine of information.

The following list of resources contain many more helpful tools, tips, and techniques for searching the Internet. If you have specific academic needs, many of these tools are what you'll want to use.

Librarians's Index to the Internet
http://lii.org/

Nueva School Search Strategy Planner
http://www.nueva.pvt.k12.ca.us/~debbie/library/research/adviceengine.html

NoodleQuest Search Tools
http://www.noodletools.com/noodlequest/

Using Internet and Web Search Engines Effectively
An Online Course from the American Library Association
http://www.ala.org/ICONN/advancedcourses.html

Search Engines

A more direct approach to finding information on the Web is to use a search engine, which is a program that runs a search while you wait for the results. Many search engines can be found on the Web. Some Web search engines are commercial and may charge you a fee to run a search. Search engines are also available for other parts of the Internet: Archie, Veronica, and Jughead are examples of such search engines.

As mentioned earlier, Yahoo! has a useful search engine. Another search engine that is used frequently is called Lycos (**http://www.lycos.com**). It's simple to operate but, as with any search tool, it takes practice and patience to master. Take the time now to connect to Lycos, and we'll take it for a test run. When you first see the opening page, you'll notice that it is very complex. But it's an excellent resource, and the instructions on the page will tell you almost everything you need to know. To search, enter a word into the white text-entry box and press the submit button. Lycos will refer back to its database of information and return to you a page of hyperlinked resources to various sites on the Internet that contain your search word.

When you type in a word or category to search, you'll notice that some of your results don't seem to apply to your topic. This is one of the pitfalls of search engines. They are very fast, but they don't think—that is your job. A search using the term "coral reef" is just as likely to turn up a link to Jimmy Buffett's Coral Reefer Band as a link to coral reef research. To perform an effective search, you will need to spend time *before* the search preparing a search strategy. When you do research using an automated tool like a search engine, you can expect many links to be unrelated to your topic of interest—but all in all, search engines are still very powerful tools.

Another type of search service that you'll hear much about is called a meta-search service. This type of service will send your query out to a number of different search engines and then tabulate the results for you. Meta-searches come in many different levels of sophistication and they also generate a large amount of information. If you're not intimidated by volume then give one of them a try.

Here's a meta-search tool that is both fun to use and powerful. Give it a try.

Ask Jeeves   http://www.askjeeves.com

One last word on search engines. These tools don't directly search the Internet. They actually search a database that is derived from the Internet. Here is how it works: Search engines use robots (automated programming tools) that search for and categorize information. This information is placed into a database. It is this database that you search when you use the search engine. Can you think of a potential problem with this system? Unfortunately, the quality of the database depends on the effectiveness of the robot that assembles the database. This is why you should not rely on just one search-engine tool. Use several because what one does not find, another might. You shouldn't have trouble finding other search engines if you don't like the ones we list here. Both of the major browsers now include a basic menu button that will connect you to a large collection of different search engines.

The following resources will help you learn more about searching the Internet.

How To Search the Web from Palomar College
http://daphne.palomar.edu/TGSEARCH

Search Engine Watch
http://searchenginewatch.com
http://searchenginewatch.com/resources/tutorials.html

Search Guide
http://www.searchengineguide.org

Meta-Search Engines Guide
http://www.hampton.lib.nh.us/srchtool/recmetaengines.htm

Chapter 2

Staying In Touch

Although the Internet is sometimes thought of as a flashy, graphically rich waste of time, it began as a tool to enable researchers to communicate between research labs across the United States. If you look at its basic features, the Internet is still a valuable and effective tool for communication. In essence, one goal of the Internet has been to eliminate the hindrance of geography on the free exchange of ideas. Whether it becomes a waste of time or a time-saving tool is entirely up to you. We hope the following ideas will help you make the most of the Internet as a tool for communication and collaboration.

A Mailbox In Cyberspace

An e-mail account is the most basic of methods for planting yourself in the Internet community. Do you have one? Don't worry if you don't. We have a number of simple, inexpensive, and fast solutions you may want to consider.

There are a few options available to you. You may be able to apply for an e-mail account through your college. If your college doesn't provide student e-mail accounts, then e-mail service through an Internet Service Provider (ISP) is a second option. ISPs require you to subscribe (meaning spend money) to acquire their service. The nature of service, hourly or monthly, will depend on your anticipated use. Although you will need to pay a fee for the service, there is an advantage because you can expect help from time to time, which you are not as likely to receive from other options.

Should you wish to pursue this option—and if you have the cash—you can find a national list of ISPs at the following address: **http://www.boardwatch.com**. Costs average about $20 per month depending on the services that you use. We suggest that you do not sign a long-term contract with an ISP until you are certain that you are happy with the service that particular provider offers. Most providers offer a free trial period before any formal commitment is necessary. Test the system at various times during the day to be certain that sufficient access is provided.

A third option, which is increasing in popularity, is to choose a free e-mail service provided by one of the many online companies. Yes, a free e-mail account with many of the bells and whistles found in a regular e-mail account can be yours for the asking. If you choose a free e-mail service, then read the fine print and understand what it means to you. In most cases, the service is provided to you free because the provider is making its money by selling advertising space to other companies. This is the same way that search engine companies and television stations make their money. In order to read your mail, you have to wade through a few commercials prominently posted on your e-mail reader. An additional condition of these free e-mail accounts is that they will gather information about you in order to customize and target the display of commercials for you. In most cases, this information is used only to target you with commercials, but always read the fine print.

The following are only a few of the more prominent services offering free e-mail and free Internet access in general. Read the fine print in their service agreements, and choose the one that offers you the most. Also, don't be afraid to change services if you're not getting what you expect.

E-Mail Service	Web Address
AltaVista	http://www.zdnet.com/downloads/altavista/
BlueLight	http://www.bluelight.com
Hotmail	http://www.hotmail.com
Juno	http://www.juno.com
Netscape	http://webmail.netscape.com
NetZero	http://www.netzero.com
WorldSpy	http://www.worldspy.com/freeisp/isp.html
Yahoo!	http://mail.yahoo.com

So, now that you're on your way to your own e-mail account, what are you going to do with it?

Simple Suggestions

If you wish to skip all of the instructions, here are a few suggestions to keep you out of trouble.

- Write down the user ID and password for your account. It's difficult to read your e-mail if you can't get into your account.
- Change your password periodically. Someone stealing your login information could do a number of unscrupulous things with your account and reputation.

- Don't use the same password for all of your accounts. Yes, it is much easier to remember if you do, but it is also much easier for someone else, too.
- Watch out for e-mail viruses. They are common and can unintentionally be passed through attached documents.

E-Mail and Your Instructor

E-mail is becoming a very common and popular way for students and instructors to communicate outside of class. As you progress through college, it is likely that you will have numerous e-mail exchanges with your instructors. The following should help you greatly.

- When communicating with your instructors, use correct spelling, grammar, punctuation, and clarity—just as you would with a carefully crafted letter.
- Most instructors will refrain from sending confidential information through e-mail since one can't guarantee the security of the message. Therefore, it is best not to request confidential information, exam scores, or course grades electronically.
- If you are asked to submit assignments electronically, be very careful as to the timing and the format you select.
- Smaller bits of text, such as summaries or project descriptions, can be sent in the body of the message; however, larger documents, including graphs and tables, should be sent as attachments. Your instructor will give you specific instructions about submitting such documents.
- Most instructors will have a mechanism for acknowledging receipt of important documents. If you have not received an acknowledging document, be certain to check by phone or in person with the instructor. It is the student's responsibility to be certain that all assignments are received in an acceptable form.

E-Mail Etiquette

Etiquette is especially important with e-mail communication. When engaged in a conversation, it is likely that you are also communicating information with the inflections in your voice, the expression on your face, and the posture of your body. If you take any or all of these away, there is a greater chance for miscommunication. Here are a few suggestions to help you out in the e-mail world.

- Say what you mean, say it concisely, and say it very carefully—once you've sent it, it is "there" and cannot be retrieved. We have all had to follow-up a vague or hurtful e-mail with explanations or apologies.
- Get to the point—your instructor is probably very busy and will be unwilling to read a tome. If you want to chat then we suggest a pizza.
- Use the subject line—it's a quick way to tell the other person what you want.

- Don't shoot from the hip. Sometimes normally timid people become raging bulls when online.
- Understand the distinction between Reply and Reply All on the menu bar—or you may have just sent your most passionate love-letter to a mailing list.
- Use a "smiley" when you think there is a possibility for misinterpretation—with e-mail, there is no opportunity to convey varied meanings by tone of voice or body language. :-)

This is by no means all there is to know about etiquette on the Net (nettiquette) and the ins-and-outs of e-mail, but it's a beginning. Each institution will supply more definite guidelines. Read them and follow them. The following list of URLs should help you find, understand, and use your e-mail to peak efficiency—or at least to maximum entertainment.

A Beginner's Guide to Effective Email by Kaitlin Duck Sherwood

http://www.webfoot.com/advice/email.top.html

Optimized E-Mail from 1 2 3 Promote!

http://www.123promote.com/workbook/plan1.htm

Email Etiquette from Air Canada

http://www.acra.ca/mlist/emailetiquette.htm

ICONnect Online Courses on E-Mail from the American Library Association

http://www.ala.org/ICONN/ibasics2.html

A Place To Call Home

After setting up an e-mail account, a homepage is the next logical step toward establishing yourself with an Internet presence. Considering the proliferation of personal homepages and the typical merit of their content, you might not realize the advantages that a personal homepage may offer to you. While an e-mail account offers you an identity on the Internet, a homepage offers you a central resource that is mostly under your control. As a student, you are somewhat nomadic and therefore required to work in many different locations throughout the day. A homepage can be an important central resource for your nomadic life. Your homepage could list online reference sites such as search engines, dictionaries, directories, and glossaries; a hyperlinked list of e-mail addresses for your instructors, classmates, and friends; a place where you can post shared information for your study groups; or a place to post class assignments for your instructors. In short, a homepage may be passive in nature but it can be a valuable tool for communication and it can save you a lot of time.

You have three basic options for posting and maintaining a homepage on the Internet. Your college may offer you space to post and maintain a homepage, you can subscribe to an ISP, or you can use a free service. The business model used by free e-mail services is similar to that of companies providing free homepage services. In most cases, these services have a basic format that you can occasionally add to or modify. Read the fine print to make sure you understand the agreement.

The following services enable you to set up a homepage on the Internet. Each of them offers a slightly different service, so spend a bit of time to really evaluate their offerings.

Home Page Service	Web Address
Geocities	http://www.geocities.com/join/
Microsoft	http://home.microsoft.com/
Netscape	http://my.netscape.com/
Yahoo!	http://my.yahoo.com/
NetColony	http://www.netcolony.com

Part of the fun of having a homepage is creating it to reflect your interests and personality. As you begin moving through the Web you'll notice a great variety of home pages. Some of them are not so good but a number are both expressive and functional. As you begin to design your own homepage, remember what you want it to do and say about you.

The following list of online resources should help you begin building your first homepage. With a quick search of the Internet, you will find a large number of other resources along this line. Be creative and enjoy the experience.

A Beginner's Guide to HTML

http://www.ncsa.uiuc.edu/General/Internet/WWW/HTMLPrimerAll.html

The Bare Bones Guide to HTML by Kevin Werbach

http://werbach.com/barebones/

If this isn't enough then the following sites can give you even more information on Web page design:

Internet.com   http://www.webreference.com

Art and the Zen of Web Sites	http://www.tlc-systems.com/webtips.html
Creating Killer Sites	http://www.killersites.com
WebDeveloper.com	http://www.webdeveloper.com
Web Building	http://builder.com
Web Monkey	htttp://www.hotwired.lycos.com/webmonkey

The Need for Plug-ins

Plug-ins are software programs that extend the capabilities of a particular browser in some specific manner, giving you the opportunity to play audio samples or view movies from within the browser. Such plug-ins are usually "cross platform" in that they can be used on Macintosh or Windows systems. Below are some examples of important and popular plug-ins that you'll probably need to view the more interactive websites.

- *Flash Player* by Macromedia—This plug-in will allow you to view animation and interactive content through your browser. This interactive content includes cartoons and games from leading-edge companies like Comedy Central, Sony, and Disney. You'll also need this plug-in to view many of the science animations being developed for your books. (**http:www.flash.com**)
- *Shockwave* by Macromedia—This is the industry standard for delivering interactive multimedia, graphics, and streaming audio on the Web. Major companies like CNN, Capitol Records, and Paramount use Shockwave as their delivery system. (**http://www.macromedia.com/shockwave/download/**)
- *RealPlayer* by RealNetworks—This plug-in allows you to play audio, video, animation, and multimedia presentations on the Web. RealPlayer Plus gives sharp pictures and audio for RealAudio and RealVideo. Many popular radio and televisions shows are available on the Web if you have this plug-in. (**http://www.realplayer.com**)
- *QuickTime* by Apple Computer—This plug-in allows you to play audio/video productions and is commonly included on CDs. It is extremely common and is typically preinstalled in the recent versions of both major browsers. Upgrades are very frequent so you can always download the newest version at their website. (**http://www.apple.com/quicktime/download/**)

If you wish to download these or other plug-ins, then you can go directly to the company that makes them or to the download gallery of the browser that you use. Both major browsers provide a listing of plug-ins by category for your

11

access. Simply download the one you want and then follow the installation instructions.

A Calendar of Events

The final step in our project to help you stay in touch with your classes, friends, and family is to make you aware of the help that a calendar program can lend. By now, it should be obvious to you that your life is not going to get less complicated. Having a tool to help you schedule your time and remember important events will be a distinct asset. Developing a routine to organize your life is the first and best step to take. The second step is to find a tool to help you remember your reading and homework assignments, library time, class schedules, exams, study-group meetings, and office hours for your instructors—in addition to all of your personal commitments.

In addition to offering you free e-mail, Yahoo!, Netscape, and many other companies offer a free online calendar service. The service is free—provided you register. By now you should be familiar with the model. The service is free to you, but you'll need to provide them with some basic personal information and you will need to endure the targeted commercials embedded in your calendar viewer. With this service, you will be able to populate a calendar with events that are important to you. Your calendar of events is viewable by day, week, month, or year. It will contain both a "To Do" list and a regular daily schedule. One of the potentially valuable resources is that of scheduled e-mail notes to remind you of important events. Never again do you need to suffer those nightmares of forgetting an exam. However, you do need to make the commitment to maintain the accuracy of your calendar. Additionally, if you know basic HTML, you can schedule events to include hyperlinks. These could be to references sites, assignments posted by your instructors, or to resources posted on the Companion Website for your textbook. Essentially, your calendar can be completely linked to the Internet.

Parting advice: Remember that you have the power of the purse; therefore, always look for the least expensive option, read and understand an agreement before you sign it, and enjoy your journey.

Something Called Privacy

The Internet has been moving over the last few years to increase the level of personalization that users experience when they browse. This personalization can be both good and bad—with increased personalization there is also less privacy. Information about you, and your viewing, and possibly purchase habits, is a commodity that companies want. If your likes and dislikes are known, then it is much easier to specifically market a product to you. For example, if I notice that you always come into my record store and browse through the Blues section, it is unlikely that I'll sell you something from the Sex Pistols. But I have a better chance of pulling you in if I run a special on BB King. Some companies are in the business of providing information about you and they collect this information on the Web. Read the fine print before you sign up, register, or provide your personal information to anyone or anything on the Web.

There are plenty of powerful people worried about privacy on the Internet, so we are not alone. The following Web addresses are for some of the many organizations that have dedicated themselves to securing and lobbying for Internet privacy. It might be a helpful exercise to make a visit to their site and learn more about the situation.

Privacy Organization	Web Address
Electronic Privacy Information Center	http://epic.org
Electronic Frontier Foundation	http://www.eff.org
Center for Democracy & Technology's Operation	http://opt-out.cdt.org
Junkbusters	http://www.junkbusters.com

DoubleClick is one of the leading companies that gathers information about people and their browsing habits. If you want to learn more about what they do and how to remove yourself from their observation, visit their site.

DoubleClick	http:www.doubleclick.net/ privacy_policy/privacy.htm

We're not trying to create a sense of mistrust about using the Internet. We don't want you to confuse the Internet with the X-Files. The great majority of times that you are asked to supply information on the Internet, it is safe to do so and is meant to help the requester more fully service your needs, but it pays to be informed about the issues involved.

Chapter 3

Is More Information a Plus? It Can Be

In your career as a student and eventually as a professional, you will spend a great deal of time using the Internet to communicate and find information. But can you trust the information you find? We want to give you hints about how to judge the information you receive from the Internet. *It's not more information you need, but the ability to evaluate what you already have.*

This guide explains what to do after you have retrieved information from a website. Should you believe the information? Should you rely on it? Should you use it as a basis for your statements when you speak or write?

The Internet contains approximately 800 million publicly-indexed Web pages,[1] providing access to a vast amount of information with a few clicks of a mouse. You can: make reservations to travel to Italy; read reviews and decide which books to read or movies to see; check out college descriptions of campuses and programs; read research studies and articles about topics ranging from new medical treatments to the status of women in Saudi Arabia; and enter digital libraries without leaving your chair.

Having so much information readily available is exciting. Whatever the topic, you can probably find information about it. For example, suppose that your sociology teacher has assigned a short research paper discussing a proposal to lower the legal drinking age. You do a quick search, and come across a website with the following information:

> Expecting people to wait until they are 21 to drink is unrealistic! In fact, there would be fewer problems if the minimum age were lowered. If people were allowed to drink responsibly, they wouldn't want to binge drink.

[1]Steve Lawrence & C. Lee Giles, *Accessibility of Information on the Web*, NATURE (1999).

You jot down some notes from this website, and then locate another relevant site, which provides the following information:

> In country after country the number of driving accidents caused by intoxication has fallen when the legal drinking age has been raised. For example, in Iceland when the legal drinking age was changed from 16 to 19, there was a 405 decline in the number of traffic deaths attributed to alcohol. The rationale for these results is clear. With increased age comes increased responsibility.

But there is a problem here. Both of these sites can't be correct. If the current minimum drinking age has been effective in lowering the number of alcohol-related accidents among people younger than 21, it can't be true that lowering the minimum drinking age will create fewer problems. Which site should we believe?

Is More Information Better Information?

The Internet is deceptive. Because it is easy to find large amounts of information, we tend to feel excited about it. But if we confuse quantity with quality, we will overlook the need to process all that information. We must choose which facts to accept and which ones to set aside as undependable.

You may have used a search engine such as Yahoo, Infoseek, or Excite. Each of these indexes approximately 16% of the 800 million pages indexed on the Internet.[2] Thus, if you conduct a search with Yahoo and another search with Excite, you will probably find two different sets of Web pages. How do we know which ones offer accurate information?

Let's return to the example of the minimum drinking-age laws. If we were to search for more information on such age laws, we would find the following pages:

- American Medical Association (**http://www.ama-assn.org**)
- Americans for a Society Free from Age Restrictions (**http://www.asfar.org**)
- Bacchus and Gamma (**http://www.bacchusgammag.org**)
- Mothers Against Drunk Driving (**http://www.madd.org**)
- National Center for Policy Analysis (**http://www.ncpa.org**)
- National Families in Action (**http://www.emory.edu/NFIA**)
- Partnership for a Drug Free America (**http://www.drugfreeamerica.org**)

But we don't know whether the information offered about minimum drinking-age laws is dependable. Furthermore, we probably wouldn't take the time to look at all of these websites. In fact, we might look at only one of the two dis-

[2]Ibid.

cussed earlier. Suppose that you looked only at the site that argues that the minimum drinking age has no basis. You would probably simply accept the information and begin to write your paper.

This example highlights an important danger of the Internet. How do you know that the author of the website is providing accurate information?

Assuming That Information is Dependable

Suppose that one morning you wake up and discover that your right eye is swollen, red, and painful. You go to the Internet to search for "eye symptoms & diagnosis." You find the following site, "Eye Disorders," where you may search by symptom. After you click on "Redness," you find the following information:

> Blepharitis is a non-specific term signifying an infection of the eyelids.
> It often develops as bacteria near the eyelid.

After reading this web page, you think you have blepharitis, so you use warm compresses to clean your eyelids. A week later, although the redness has disappeared, your eye is extremely painful and you think you have lost vision in that eye.

When we read something on the Internet, we may assume that the information is accurate and dependable. However, remember that anyone can create a web page and put it on the Internet. The author of a web page might have little or no knowledge about the topic. Thus, when you search for information about eye diseases, you might find a page written by someone who once had an eye infection and another page written by an opthamologist who has studied eye infections for twenty years. The fact that a page is on the Internet says nothing about the quality of the information there.

The authors of these sites often want you to believe that you have found the truth on their pages. They state their information without the ordinary cautions that reputable experts would provide. Therefore, it is very easy to find highly-biased information on the Internet.

If you do not question the information provided on a website, you risk accepting flawed information. In the eye-care example, you could have lost your sight by depending upon information you found on the Internet. You need to question that information. Healthy doubt is positive self-defense.

You Control Information; It Doesn't Control You

If you assume that information on the Internet is dependable, you become a passive recipient of that information. When you passively use information, it determines how you react. For example, suppose that you are exploring on the Internet and you read the following advertisement:

> Sausage is among the more healthy foods available to us. Its production
> occurs in incredibly clean factories where every safeguard is taken to

preserve the healthful benefits of meat products. In addition the hogs that provide the sausage are treated with respect for the first two years of their lives. They are fed, inoculated and pampered for it is their health and well-being that guarantees a profitable sausage industry.

If you passively accepted this information, you probably would not hesitate to buy a pound or two of sausage on your next trip to the grocery store. The information is shaping your behavior.

Certainly, some of the information on the Internet is dependable. To determine which information is dependable, you must actively reflect about whether you should accept each item as correct. In other words, you must take control of the information and use it only if it meets your standards.

If it does not meet those standards, you will want to keep looking. You might find additional information that will lead you to accept a modified version of the original information. The point is that YOU decide whether information is worthwhile. Consequently, you are in control of the information, and you therefore control your behavior.

As just noted, one way to question information you find on the Internet is to look for additional information. For example, you might want to search for a site that offers conflicting information. (Authors rarely offer links to sites that disagree with theirs.) When you search for conflicting information you are acting on the information, instead of letting the person who created a website control you.

When websites disagree, what should you do? You might begin to feel as though you will never be able to make decisions because there is so much contradictory information. Try not to feel overwhelmed; recognize your confusion is normal. You will soon learn tools that can help you decide which information to accept. For now, it is important to realize that actively searching for conflicting information is one way to question information offered on a web page.

The Need for Critical Thinking

As stated earlier, when you assume that information is dependable, you risk accepting flawed information. What are the consequences of accepting and using flawed information? First, you might include flawed information in a paper. If your teacher is aware of this, you might get a lower grade. Second, you might use flawed information when making choices as a consumer. This could hurt you financially. For example, suppose that a website reports that a certain stock is sure to provide high returns. Your grandparents use their life savings to buy this stock. However, the information on the website is incorrect, and your grandparents lose all their money. A third possible consequence of relying on incorrect information is that your health might be damaged, as in the eye-care example given earlier.

To control the information you encounter on the Internet, you must actively question it. Looking for additional information is one tool for doing so. This book provides several other tools that will enable you to *think critically* about information on the Internet.

Critical thinking is the process of using a set of critical questions to evaluate information. In the following chapters, you will learn a set of questions that you can use in deciding whether you should accept or reject the information you encounter on the Internet. Asking these questions is a powerful strategy for distinguishing clear thinking from sloppy thinking. You are not using critical thinking to find "right" or "wrong" information regarding an issue. Instead, you will be using critical questions to find accurate or reasonable information.

Chapter 4

What Argument Does the Site Make?

One of the most popular diet plans on the market today is the "high-protein diet" that requires the dieter to eat large amounts of protein and almost no carbohydrates. If you wanted to determine the medical support for such a diet, you could hop on the Web to find research.

After a bit of searching, you may come upon a site with the following information:

> By limiting carbohydrates, the body reduces its insulin output, and large amounts of protein trigger the body to release fat.

After searching a few more sites, you may find another site with this conflicting information:

> The weight lost by high-protein diets is only water weight. This diet plan is *incredibly* unhealthy!

These two Web pages come to different conclusions about whether eating lots of lean protein will help you lose fat. So how do we come to a well-informed conclusion about this diet plan? With whom should we agree? We could look for additional information on health sites, like **http://www.awesomebody.com**, or news sites like **http://www.cbs2.com**. Both pages offer information that will help us understand the complexity of the issue. Instead of claiming that this diet is either helpful or harmful, these sites offer information supporting the idea that this diet plan is helpful in certain respects and harmful in other respects. Instead of concluding that this form of dieting is all bad or all good, we can conclude that in some ways it is bad while in other ways it is good.

It is often easy to find information on the Internet that suggests that certain ideas are all good or all bad. Someone who claims that an idea is all good or all bad probably has not looked at all the relevant evidence. In fact, it is nearly impossible to gather all the evidence regarding an idea. Because ideas are complex, they usually have both good and bad aspects. You must realize that an idea is usually somewhere in the middle of good and bad. It is your responsibility to evaluate what ways an idea is somewhat good and somewhat bad. This chapter will teach you to begin this evaluation.

In Chapter 1 you learned the importance of questioning the information you find on the Internet. But what information should you question? You might locate a website that has six pages of text. You don't have the time or the interest to question every sentence in those six pages. But it isn't necessary to question every sentence. Instead, you need to identify the author's argument and apply critical thinking skills to it.

An **argument** is an author's conclusion plus the reasons offered in support of that conclusion. Thus, when we say that critical thinking is an evaluation of an argument, we mean that it is an evaluation of the conclusion and the reasons for it. Let's break down that definition into its components.

Identifying the Conclusion

A **conclusion** is the point that the author wants you to accept. It is generally the author's opinion, and his or her reason for trying to communicate with you is to share that opinion. To identify the conclusion, you ask, "What is the main point?" Identifying the conclusion of a passage is an extremely important, yet somewhat difficult, task.

Here are some hints for finding the conclusion:

1 When reading a passage, you should repeatedly think to yourself, "What is the author's main point? What idea or position does she want me to accept?"
2 You will often find a conclusion at the beginning or end of a passage. While you should think about the author's main point while you are reading the whole passage, focus on the first and last paragraphs.
3 Look for ideas that seem to be defending, or arguing for, other ideas. The ideas being supported will be conclusions.
4 Look for words that suggest that a conclusion is coming, such as the following:

You might already happen to agree with an author's conclusion. However, you need to set aside your own views momentarily. Your emotional attachment to an idea is not a good basis for accepting or rejecting an author's position. Before you decide to accept a conclusion, you need to identify the reasons offered in support of that conclusion. Let's practice identifying the conclusion of a passage that you might find at a website.

Are wedding coordinators really necessary? Many people claim they cost more than they are worth, but my experience tells me that those people are wrong. Most people struggle with planning a wedding because they've never had to plan anything like this before. They need someone who is experienced. That's where wedding coordinators come in. They know who to work with, the proper etiquette, and how to match wedding plans to your budget.

The author's main point—the conclusion—is that you should hire a wedding coordinator when planning a wedding. The author doesn't use those exact words. However, she tries to convince you of the usefulness of wedding coordinators, thus implicitly supporting the belief that wedding coordinators are needed. You have learned how to identify part of an argument. Now, let's look at the second part: the reasons.

Identifying the Reasons

A *reason* is an explanation for why we should accept a certain conclusion. It answers the question "Why?". Reasons establish the credibility of the conclusion. We decide whether to reject or accept a conclusion based on the reasons.

Many types of ideas can be reasons. Reasons can be personal testimonials, research findings, beliefs, or any other statements that offer support for a conclusion. Think of reasons as sawhorses that support a piece of wood (the conclusion). Without the sawhorses, the board would fall. Similarly, without good reasons a conclusion will fall. Your identification and evaluation of reasons will largely determine whether you accept the author's conclusion.

Suppose that an author concludes that parents should carefully monitor their children's use of the Internet. You want to find out why the author came to that conclusion. To find the reasons offered, ask, "*Why* should parents monitor their kids' Internet exploration?"

When you identify reasons, you need to identify anything the author offers to support her conclusion. For now, we are not concerned with the *quality* of the reasons. You might think that some of the reasons the author provides are pretty poor. However, if the author believes that something is a reason, you must identify it as such. You will be able to evaluate that reason *after* you have completely identified the argument.

In the same way that there are certain words that suggest that a conclusion is coming, there are also words that suggest that the author is offering a reason. The best reason indicator word is "because."

REASON INDICATOR WORDS

Also   as a result of   because   first.... second
for example   for one thing   in addition

Where Do I Find Arguments?

You can find arguments everywhere. When you listen to television commercials, talk with friends, or read almost anything on the Internet, you will find that someone is presenting an argument. That person is trying to persuade you of something. Remember, however, that a belief or opinion presented without reasons is not an argument. Arguments include both a conclusion and reasons supporting it.

Let's practice identifying the argument of a passage you might find on the Web. Look at this movie review for "The Blair Witch Project":

> After the "Blair Witch Project" hit the big screens, Hollywood was abuzz with talk about this low-budget blockbuster. Many even argued that this was one of the scariest movies of all time. I, on the other hand, do not understand what is causing such a commotion. The Blair Witch Project was incredibly slow, not entertaining, and far from scary.
>
> Most of the movie was simply kids walking around through the woods. How is that scary? There was almost no tension or suspense until the very end of the film. This movie definitely did not live up to my expectations. After all the hype created surrounding this movie, I was expecting an entertaining and scary movie. That is not what I saw.

The reviewer is making an argument. He is trying to convince you of something. There are no clear indicator words to lead you to the conclusion; however, you can infer that the author is trying to convince you that you should not see the movie.

Conclusion: You should not see "The Blair Witch Project."

Why does the author believe that you should not see the movie? Now you are trying to identify the reasons he offers in support of his conclusion. Remember, we are looking for statements that answer the question, "Why shouldn't you see the movie?"

Reason: The movie is not entertaining.

The reviewer believes that you should not see the movie because he wasn't entertained. Is that the only reason the author believes that you shouldn't see the movie? The fact that he didn't think the movie is entertaining is the main reason he thinks you shouldn't see the movie. However, he tells you *why* he thinks that the movie is not entertaining. He offers reasons that support his main reason.

Supporting Reason: The movie is not scary; it is incredibly slow.

The author explicitly states that the movie is not scary. He points out that the majority of the film was simply the actors and actresses walking through the woods. If the entire movie had been like the ending, then the movie would have been scary.

You have now identified the argument made by the reviewer. You identified the conclusion the author offered as well as the reasons he provided in support of his conclusion. Now what? At this time, all you should be doing is learning to identify arguments. You will soon learn how to use critical questions to determine the value of the information. But before you can do any kind of evaluation, you need to make sure that you have correctly identified the author's argument. The next chapter will build on the ability to identify the arguments presented on websites. Its purpose is to sensitize you to the importance of the source of the information on a site.

Chapter 5

What is the Source of the Information?

While searching the Internet, you come across this information at **http://www.netspace.org/ herald/issues/100397/speech.f.html**:

> Many arguments for speech restrictions deny that hateful speech is protected by the Constitution. Such arguments are based on the fact that hate speech does not advance the spirit of free speech. An essay written by judge and lawyer Simon Rifkind emphasizes this point. Fighting words are unprotected because they do not advance the civil discourse, which the First Amendment is designed to promote Rifkind said. A university is a very special community. Speech which is not civil is at odds with the purpose of the campus.

But after you bookmark this site, you find another site about affirmative action that presents you with this conflicting information:

> Free speech is protected under our Constitution. The First Amendment protects our speech—even if it is offensive. Adopting speech codes is the same thing as censorship, and this is in violation of the Constitution.

> How much should college students be allowed to say on campus? When, if ever, is speech not protected by the Constitution? Is hate speech protected by the Constitution? College administrators throughout the country are heavily debating these issues. Because of this, many Web pages have important things to say about this issue. However, as we said

in Chapter 1, it is rare to find a site that presents multiple views on an issue. If we want to find different views, we must go out and find them.

Where might we look to find more information about freedom of speech? For starters, this is an issue that many civil liberties groups are interested in. Many of these groups, such as the ACLU, believe that by regulating any kind of speech, schools will be taking away the civil rights of their students. We might also look for information on university Web pages, or on pages designed by organizations that fight against hate speech and hate crimes. Here are some websites that have information relevant to this issue.

- Free Speech Movement Archives (**http://www.fsm-a.org**)
- Justice on Campus (**http://joc.mit.edu**)
- Public Interest Research Groups (**http://www.pirg.org**)
- The Ethical Spectacle (**http://www.spectacle.org**)

One way to sort through the information is to equip yourself with tools for evaluating the reliability of the source. That is the goal of this chapter.

The Importance of the Information Provider

Web pages originate from diverse sources, and the quality of the information they provide varies greatly. Some are much more objective, accurate, comprehensive, and up-to-date than others. Therefore, you should rely much more on some sources than on others.

Variability in the quality of sources is not unique to the Web. It is also characteristic of more traditional sources of information, such as newspapers, television, and magazines. We know, for example, that we ought to pay more attention to claims made in *The New York Times* than to those made in the *National Inquirer*. In such cases, however, we can usually determine pretty easily just what the source is. The source of information and the credibility of that source are much harder to discern on the Internet. Fewer and less obvious clues are available, and there are no accepted standards for presenting material online. Thus, some websites can be trusted much more than others. The first critical-thinking question we need to ask about a Web page is: *What is the source and what do we know about it?*

Differences Among Sources of Information

Sources of information vary in many ways. In some cases we can determine a great deal about the source; in others, very little information about the source is provided. The best websites provide extensive information. Among the things you want to know about a source are: *its motives, its content quality, and its record of past performance.*

Motives

Websites exist because someone wants them there, not because any independent judge has determined them worthy of inclusion. Their motives and purposes vary greatly, and these differences greatly affect the quality of the information. You therefore need to ask, What is the major motivation behind this site? Is it to inform, to persuade, to sell, to entertain, or to accomplish something else? Knowing the motives behind the site's creation helps you better judge its content. Knowing its motives should also remind you to ask, What is not being said?

To determine the likely motives of website sponsors, you need to ask who sponsored the site and what they say about themselves. Sites vary greatly in how clear and accessible they make this information. Try to obtain the following kinds of information about the site's sponsor:

- The name of the organization or individual responsible for the site.
- Links to additional information about the organization or individual responsible.
- A clear statement of the site's goals.
- A clear indication of any sponsors of the site and whether they are profit or nonprofit. For example, the statement "Funded by the National Institute of Mental Health" clearly indicates a nonprofit sponsor.
- A link to the homepage of the site.
- Links to other important information related to the site, such as a table of contents or bibliographies.

Once you have a good sense of the website sponsor, you should ask: What are the likely motives of the source? Some common motives are:

- To Inform
- To advocate
- To sell
- To provide news
- To express individual opinions
- Mixed motives

Let us take a closer look at each of these.

To Inform

The purpose of many websites is to present information relevant to a particular topic. Online library sources and government agencies, for example, are informational. These are likely to be the least biased sources. Many URL addresses that end in **.edu** or **.gov** tend to be informational sources because they are sponsored by educational institutions or by government agencies. Examples of materials found on informational pages include:

- Government statistics
- Information about careers
- Research results
- Directories of businesses

Each of the following sites is primarily informational:

http://lcweb.loc.gov (Library of Congress)

http://www.epa.gov (U.S. Environmental Protection Agency)

http://www.ukans.edu/history/vl/ (History Index)

http://www.utm.edu/research/iep (The Internet Encyclopedia of Philosophy)

http://www.doc.gov (U.S. Department of Commerce)

To Advocate

An advocacy page is sponsored by an organization or individual that seeks to influence the opinions of those who access the site. Its purpose is to persuade you. Such pages therefore reflect strong biases, which you need to identify in judging the quality of the information.

Advocacy URL addresses often end in **.org** if they are sponsored by a nonprofit organization. Political parties and self-help groups are examples of advocacy organizations. The following clues suggest an advocacy motivation:

- Seeking of financial donations
- Promotion of a cause
- Efforts to recruit members to an organization
- Provision of ways for like-minded people to pursue further contact

Each of the following is an advocacy site:

http://www.plannedparenthood.org (Planned Parenthood)

http://www.nra.org (National Rifle Association)

http://www.now.org (National Organization for Women)

http://www.cc.org (Christian Coalition)

http://aclu.org (American Civil Liberties Union)

To Sell

The primary purpose of many sources is to promote or sell products or services. Thus, you need to be especially alert to biases in information provided by such sites. Virtually everything that is sold in stores is now sold on the Web, including books, appliances, drugs, and clothing. URL addresses whose purpose is to sell often end in **.com**. Following are examples of sites whose main motivation is to sell:

> **http://www.amazon.com**
> **http://www.ebay.com**
> **http://www.cdnow.com**
> **http://www.gap.com**
> **http://www.circuitcity.com**

To Provide News

The primary purpose of many websites is to provide current information on diverse issues. Some such sites are simply postings of news from traditional print sources such as *The New York Times, USA Today, Newsweek,* and *Time.* The purpose of some news sites (e.g., Slate.com and Salon.com) is to try to integrate the information from multiple news sites. Examples of news sites include the following:

> **http://www.nytimes.com** (New York Times)
> **http://www.usatoday.com** (USA Today)
> **http://www.newsweek.com** (Newsweek)
> **http://www.wsj.com** (The Wall Street Journal)

To Express Individual Opinions

Many people create a website as a way to express themselves. They may want to express personal ideas—works of art or poetry, for example—or to pursue hobbies. Some site creators enjoy expressing provocative criticism of existing institutions. Some simply want to "blow their own horn." Personal opinion Web pages are highly diverse and are likely to be very biased. Find out as much as you can about the person behind the site to decide how much attention you should pay to the opinions expressed. Examples of such sites include:

> **http://hometown.aol.com/mwsneaka/index.html**
> **http://hometown.aol.com/aaofvalues/abortion.htm**
> **http://ljh.www.cistron.nl/laurens/**

Mixed Motives

Websites often reflect multiple motives. Be especially alert to sites that suggest one motive (such as informing) but actually reflect other important motives (such as selling). For example, sites that combine the information and selling motives are likely to be less objective than those whose sole motive is to provide

28

information. Another common practice is to make a website look as though it is informing when in fact it is also advocating.

You need to be alert to any motives that bias information on a website. Pay particular attention to the role of advertising and sponsors. Try to determine whether they might be influencing the content of a site. For example, if you are seeking information for a paper on gun control, you should be suspicious of sites sponsored by the National Rifle Association and sites advertising guns, as well as sites sponsored by anti-gun groups.

Noting who is advertising on a website provides you important clues to possible biases. Also, when accessing sites that look like information sites, check the backgrounds of contributors to that site. Do they reflect particular political biases? Are they associated with organizations noted for advocating particular points of view? This information is essential for determining the credibility of the source.

Content Quality

The quality of information available at websites varies greatly. Sometimes you find "garbage," at other times "gold." You need to ask several questions to assess the quality of information at a site. The most informative sites are ones that are *scholarly, logically organized, broad in scope,* and *up to date.*

How Scholarly is the Web Site?

The following questions help establish the scholarliness of a website:

- *Do the Web pages reflect authorities that are known for their expertise in the areas in which they write?*
- *Does the site emphasize primary sources when appropriate?* Primary sources are original pieces of work, such as research studies in periodicals or essays presenting an original theory.
- *How scholarly are the secondary sources?* Secondary sources are those in which someone other than the originator of the information interprets it. Stories reported in news magazines, such as *Time* and *Newsweek*, are usually secondary sources. Critical reviews of original research published in reputable journals tend to be high-quality secondary sources, as do book chapters that summarize research findings. The most informative secondary sources are those that refer extensively to primary sources and also critically evaluate such sources. If you are working on a research project, it is usually desirable to include reputable primary sources. By the time information has been reported by a secondary source, it is likely to have been filtered through a number of biases. The best secondary sources are those that give you enough information about the primary sources to make your own judgments.
- *Does the website evaluate its information prior to posting it?* Some sites "let anything in," while others are much more selective. Selective sites pay close attention

to the authority's credentials and often provide extensive information about them.

- *Is the information at the site presented at a sufficiently high level of complexity, or has important information been lost for the sake of simplicity?* One way to determine the complexity of information is to ask whether it is intended for the general public or for a more select or informed audience. You should seek information that is presented at a level of complexity suitable for your purpose.

How Well Organized is the Website?

Web page information can be best understood if it fits into a coherent overall structure. Thus, you should ask the following questions about the organization of a site:

- Is the organizational logic clear?
- Is it easy to determine its contents and links and how they are related?
- Does the design of the site allow easy and understandable navigation?
- Is it clear what is an advertisement and what is not and how the advertisements are related to the site?

How Comprehensive is the Website?

The highest-quality websites tend to be most thorough. So you want to ask of a site:

- What is its scope?
- Does it have a large number of relevant links?
- Does it omit important information?
- Does it present multiple perspectives on an issue?

How Current is the Information?

An advantage of the Web is that it can make new information available very quickly. Because of the rapid reproduction of information, most Web sources need to update information frequently. Thus, you need to ask these questions about a site:

- Are its references or bibliographies "cutting edge?"
- What process does the source use to update its information?
- What is the most recent update?

Look for clues to evaluate the quality of a site's content. You can obtain evaluative information from Web-based subject directories, organizations' membership directories, and magazine articles rating websites. One excellent source, which first appeared in the journal *College and Research Libraries News* in February 1994, is a column called "Internet Reviews." It provides evaluative information concerning website content. In addition, an ongoing series of articles ("Internet Resources") in the same publication lists Internet sites that provide information on subjects such as law, health and medicine, and economics. Columns similar to "Internet Reviews" can be found in *Library Journal.*

Past Performance

Like the brand names of cars, clothing, or appliances, websites develop reputations based on their perceived performance. If a website provides high-quality information, the word gets around. You should be alert to clues about a site's past performance. For example, do you encounter frequent references to the site? Have claims posted on the site held up over time, or have other sites frequently corrected them? Has the site gained a reputation for reporting false rumors? Do your instructors think highly of the site because of their prior experience with it? Ask people whom you respect about their favorite sites. Be sure to ask them why they like the site. If they give you good reasons, you can bookmark such sites.

Responding to Information from Unknown Sources

Sometimes the information available at a website is so limited that you can't determine its source. In other cases, you know who wrote it, but that is all you know.

What should you do? First, look for helpful links. For example, is there a link to a homepage that might provide a clue to the author's name, qualifications, or purpose for writing the piece? Does the URL provide a clue about the origin of the page? If you can't get further information, look for other sites. Eliminating sites whose source is unknown should speed up your search for high-quality information. There are likely to be many relevant sites whose sources you can determine. Spend your time with the sites that are most likely to provide high-quality information.

In general, you want to locate sites with the following characteristics:

- There is information about the purpose or motivation of the site.
- The page clearly indicates who is responsible for the information.
- Multiple contact points are listed that can be used to verify the site's legitimacy.
- There is a link to the homepage of the person or organization responsible for the site.
- Sponsors or advertisers are clearly indicated.
- Other links are provided to help users learn more about what is included at the site.

Chapter 6

How Dependable is the Authority who Provided This Information?

At **http://www.meyers-briggs.com/relationships.html** you will find this information:

> We are naturally attracted to individuals who are different from ourselves—and therefore somewhat exciting.

After searching a few more sites, you will eventually find a site with an argument similar to the following:

> We are likely to pursue a lover that is similar to us because likes attract. We want someone with the same interests and the same background. It is difficult for a relationship to succeed if the partners have little in common.

> How many times have you heard the phrase "opposites attract?" Probably just as many times as you have heard the phrase "birds of a feather flock together." How can we decide which one to believe? Although it may seem safe to find the answer in scientific studies, even people whom we would expect to have much expertise, such as Ph.D. psychologists, disagree about such issues. Where do we go from here? You guessed it! Search for more information. You will most likely find even more "experts" with *different* conclusions about this issue. How do you know which experts to believe? This chapter will provide you with the tools you need to determine which experts are most dependable.

If you were trying to obtain additional information about whether opposites attract, one strategy is to ask, "What do other experts have to say about this?" However, experts disagree. Moreover, like the rest of us, experts are often biased and their biases may influence their conclusions.

Because experts disagree and are fallible, we need to apply our critical-thinking filters to their opinions. If we ask the right questions, we will find that some authorities possess much more expertise than others and therefore that some opinions should be more trusted than others. Consequently, one of the most important questions to ask about a webpage is "How dependable is the author of the page?" or "How much should I trust what the author has to say?"

A Special Case

The books, journals, and other resources in your college library have been evaluated to some degree—usually by a librarian or some other procedure set up by the library. Indexes and databases have usually been evaluated according to an established set of procedures or rules. In addition, articles in many journals and periodicals have been refereed (evaluated by experts) before being published. You therefore have good reason to trust information in these sources.

When you use the Web, no such evaluation has taken place. There are no governing bodies or evaluative standards. The Web is much like a magazine section in a local grocery store whose owner allows anyone in town to print a magazine and place it on rack. This analogy should help you see clearly that the ease of publishing documents on the Web results in the availability of information from authors with widely varying levels of expertise. The most reliable authorities are just a click away from the most dubious ones. The burden is on you, the user, to evaluate such authorities.

Criteria For Choosing Among Authorities

When we appeal to authorities for information, we are appealing to sources— experts—that are supposed to know more than most of us about a given topic. We believe that experts have access to certain facts and have special qualifications for drawing conclusions from those facts. You will encounter many kinds of "authorities" on the Web. Here are a few examples:

> Movie reviewers: "One of the ten best movies of the year." Valerie Viewer, *Toledo Gazette*
> Organizations: "The American Medical Association supports this position."
> Researchers: "Studies show..."

How do you choose which authorities to trust? When you look for information, you need to know the basis of the author's authority. Following are a number of questions you can ask to answer the question, "How dependable is the authority?"

Is the Authority Well-Known and Well-Regarded?

Have you encountered the name frequently in your readings or studies? Has your professor referred to the name in a positive fashion?

What are the Authority's Credentials?

What is the author's position, institutional affiliation, and address? What organizations does she belong to? What has she done to demonstrate extensive expertise in the area in which she is writing? Has the person had extensive experience related to the topic?

There are several ways to get information relevant to this question. First, you can check the webpage you are reading for biographical information and, if the information is not there, check links to other documents. You can also check the author's homepage.

If such checks don't work, you might try to contact the author directly to request further information about her work and professional background. Often, for example, you can obtain the author's e-mail address. You will not always receive a reply to an e-mail message, but when you do, it can be very helpful. What you are trying to discover is evidence that this expert has studied the topic thoroughly and carefully and has been judged by others to have achieved some expertise in this area.

Was the Authority in a Position to Have Especially Good Access to Pertinent Facts?

Was the author a firsthand observer of the events about which she makes claims? Has a newspaper reporter actually witnessed an event, or has she merely relied on reports from others? If the authority is not a firsthand observer, whose claims is she repeating? Why should we rely on those claims? In general, you should be more impressed by primary sources than by secondary sources.

Has the Authority Been Screened By Some Organization?

You can ask a number of questions to discern whether the author's essay has gone through some kind of screening or refereeing process to verify that it meets the standards or aims of some external evaluating body.

1. *Is the name of any organization given on the document?* Are there clues on the headers or footers that show that the document is part of a reputable academic or scholarly web site? If not, are there links to other sites that provide such information?
2. *Is the organization well recognized in the relevant field of study, and is it the appropriate one for judging the content in the document?*

What Are the Likely Biases?

Is there good reason to believe that the authority is relatively free of distorting influences? Factors that can influence how evidence is reported are personal needs, prior expectations, general beliefs, attitudes, values, theories, and ideologies. These can subconsciously or deliberately affect how evidence is presented. We can't expect any authority to be totally unbiased. We can, however, expect less bias from some authorities than from others, and we can try to determine whether bias is present by seeking information about the authority's personal interest in the topic under discussion. For example, we want to be especially wary if an authority stands to benefit financially from the actions she advocates.

Authorities do not present pure facts or totally objective arguments. The information they present has been actively selected and constructed. The popularity of the Web makes it a perfect outlet for publishing documents influenced by business, social, political, and personal interests, and as a result much of the information available on the Web reflects biased uses of data. Check for biases by asking the following questions:

1. *Is the author representing any organizations that are likely to have biased agendas?* For example, is a corporation, or a "think tank" with strong political views, sponsoring the author's point of view, rather than a university or a government agency? Does the URL reveal any clues about organizations that may be sources of bias?
2. *What kinds of positions has the author taken in the past?* Do they reveal a particular set of values or perspectives?

How Scholarly and Fair Has the Author Been?

This is one of most important questions you can ask! You can evaluate the author's scholarship or relevant knowledge in the area under discussion asking the following questions:

1. *Does the author refer to or show knowledge of related sources, with appropriate citations?*
2. *Does the author display knowledge of theories or research methods that are usually considered relevant in the treatment of this topic?*
3. *If claims need empirical support, does the author provide research evidence for them?*
4. *If the author is treating a controversial topic, does she acknowledge this and present arguments on multiple sides of the issue, or is the presentation very one-sided?*
5. *If it is a research document, has the author provided sufficiently detailed information about the nature of the methodology and the actual findings of the studies?*
6. *Does the author evaluate the information he presents? Does the author critically evaluate his own position?*
7. *Does the author anticipate and answer counterarguments and possible objections?*

8. *Does the document include a full bibliography, and does the bibliography contain references to high-quality sources, including primary sources and recent scholarly reviews?*
9. *Does the document show evidence that the writer is up-to-date on the topic? Do cited sources show recent dates? Does the document show a "last updated" date?*

Our Inescapable Dependence on Authorities

By now you should be sensitized to the need to avoid uncritically accepting what experts have to say. However, we all must rely on experts. When a plane crashes, violence erupts, a new epidemic occurs, or we have to decide whether we need surgery for a physical ailment, we do not have the time or resources to become an expert on these issues. We frequently need the best answers we can get as quickly as possible. Thus, we cannot avoid some dependence on authorities.

We have to make decisions that require authoritative input. Knowing that some experts are much better than others is a good starting point in making such decisions. Carefully selecting which authorities to pay most attention to is a good second step. Learning to ask the critical questions that we discuss in subsequent sections of this book should also help you decide. We encourage you to be skeptical and selective, but ultimately to be decisive.

Chapter 7

What Does the Information Mean?

At **http://www.ceousa.org/** we find this argument:

> Affirmative action today has strayed from its original intent and has become largely a program to confer special benefits on designated groups. The objective is no longer to guarantee equal opportunity but to achieve equal results. The focus is no longer on individuals but groups. And the end justifies whatever means are necessary, including the use of double standards based on race, ethnicity, and gender. What is more, many of the beneficiaries of affirmative action programs today are middle class or even affluent members of preferred racial and ethnic groups.

It will not take you very long to find another site with the following argument:

> Affirmative Action protects equal opportunity. It is the best solution we have in our country for removing discrimination.

> Should businesses and schools be required to hire and accept certain numbers of minorities? Is this the only safeguard minorities have against discrimination? Are there better alternatives? People have come to many different conclusions on this issue. Because of this, websites dealing with the issue often contradict one another.

> Again, the first step we must take in coming to a well-informed conclusion is to search for more information. Here is a list of Web pages where you may find information about affirmative action:

- American Association for Affirmative Action (**http://www.affirmativeaction.org/**)
- Californians against Discrimination and Preferences (CADAP) (**http://www.cadap.org**)
- Center for Individual Rights (CIR) (**http://www.cir-usa.org**)
- Defend Affirmative Action Party (**http://www.umich.edu/~daap/**)

All of these sites contain large amounts of information about affirmative action. In fact, if one were to read through all the information on these sites, one might end up more confused than before. Some of this confusion is caused by the fact that authors of websites rarely define key words or phrases within their arguments. This chapter will help you to identify words and phrases that must be defined before you, as a critical thinker, can accept or reject the argument.

Words May Have More Than One Meaning

Think about the word "success." What does it mean to you? Does it mean getting good grades in school? Does it mean making a tremendous amount of money? Does it mean being content in your job? Because language is complex, "success" could mean any of those things. Most words or phrases have multiple meanings.

If you looked up a word in a dictionary, you would likely encounter a variety of meanings for it. For example, when "run" is used as a verb, it has about fifteen meanings. If it is used as a noun, it has about twelve meanings. As an adjective, it has at least three meanings.

Suppose that you read the phrase "censoring the Internet" on a Web page. What does the author mean? Does the "Internet" mean the World Wide Web? Could it refer to electronic mail? Moreover, what type of censorship is the author referring to? Who is doing the censoring? The author knows exactly what she means by the phrase, yet these questions demonstrate that you, the reader, do not know what the author means.

When you search for information on the Internet, you will undoubtedly encounter words and phrases that have various meanings. Consequently, you need to be aware of the potential confusion associated with words and phrases.

The Need to Discover Meaning

You should be concerned about multiple meanings because they can have a serious impact on your willingness to accept an argument. You cannot respond to information unless you understand the author's intention in using a word or phrase.

Suppose that you are writing a paper about home schooling for your education class. You search for "home schooling" on the Internet and find an article, "Home Schooled Students Accepted at Universities." You read the first paragraph.

> Home schooling is becoming more and more popular throughout America. Although many would think that home-schooled children have a disadvantage getting into good universities, the opposite is true. It seems that universities find home-schooled students more disciplined and more mature, and desire these students on their campus to add to the diversity of the student body.

The article seems to be concluding that home schooled students can probably get accepted at colleges and universities. But, what does the author mean by "home schooled"? Some students who are home schooled attend some classes at a junior high or high school. Other home schooled students might do all their learning at home. Could there be a difference between those two types of students? If the author is referring to students who take some classes at a junior high or high school but stay home for other classes, we might be more likely to believe that those students have an extremely good chance of getting into college. However, if a "home schooled" student does all her learning at home, we might be less likely to agree with the author's conclusion.

You have identified an important source of potential confusion. Now try to use the context of the article to determine what the author means by "home schooled." What if you cannot rely on the context for the author's meaning? If you don't know what the author means by "home schooled," you cannot accept the argument that "home schooled students have a good chance of getting into college." In other words, before you can agree or disagree with an argument, you must be sure that you understand the author's intent in using certain key words.

Making a List of Alternative Meanings

How do you find multiple meanings of words and phrases? Here are some tools for doing so:

- *Carefully read the information and identify the argument.* Remember, you want to identify the conclusion of the argument and reasons offered to support it.
- *Identify the key words in the conclusion and reasons.* Which words seem especially important? You aren't trying to identify words or phrases that simply have multiple meanings. Almost every word on a Web page has multiple meanings. Instead, you are looking for words that are central to the argument. You are trying to find words that could affect your willingness to accept the argument.
- Make a list of alternative meanings for the key words. *When you identify a key word or phrase, list different meanings, interpretations, and implications of that word or phrase. Here is an example:*

CONCLUSION: **Violence in schools** is a serious problem that warrants legislative attention.

1. **Violence in schools** could refer to the number of murders and life-threatening injuries that occur in schools because a student has engaged in some type of action to cause those injuries.
2. **Violence in schools** could refer to the murders and life-threatening injuries that occur in schools due to the actions of an outsider (e.g., an adult who opens fire on a playground).
3. **Violence in schools** could refer to the number of fistfights that occur in schools.
4. **Violence in schools** could refer to the study of violence by students in the classroom.

Based on the conclusion, "violence in schools" could take on any of the meanings just listed. We do not know which of the meanings the author intends. However, each of these meanings could affect our willingness to accept the author's conclusion.

Let's try another example. Suppose that you find the following information on pornography:

Many people argue that pornography is a victimless crime, but that is just because we can not immediately see the victim. In the end, pornography destroys the heart, mind, and soul of the individual.

The author is trying to convince us that pornography is a crime that creates victims. What words or phrases are important to the author's argument? Understanding what the author means by "pornography" and "crime" is important. "Pornography" is a very unclear word. Would the author consider a very short inexplicit sex scene in a dramatic movie to be pornographic? Does the author believe that any type of nakedness is pornographic? Alternatively, are magazines like *Playboy* considered pornography? In short, we do not know precisely what the author means by pornography. Certainly, there are various degrees of potentially pornographic materials. Depending on the degree, we might be willing to agree with the author's conclusion; however, we don't know what the author believes pornography is.

Furthermore, what does the author mean by "crime"? Generally, viewing certain types of pornography is not a crime. Thus, does the author mean that viewing pornography is a crime in the sense that the viewer is breaking a law and deserves to be punished? Alternatively, does the author mean that the viewer is committing a crime because he or she is doing something that is morally offensive? Because the author is trying to convince us that pornography is a crime, we should understand what he or she means by "crime."

Get into the habit of generating at least two possible meanings for a key word and thinking about how those meanings affect your willingness to accept the author's conclusion. Focus on key words and make a list of their potential meanings.

Use Caution When Your Meaning Differs From That of the Information-Provider

Let's return to the home schooling example. You didn't know the author's intent in using the phrase "home schooled." When you cannot determine the author's intended meaning you should be wary of relying on that information. Why?

Suppose that you went to several different websites for information to include in a paper about home schooling. Some of those websites used one definition of home schooling while others used an alternative definition. If you did not identify the differences between the definitions, your paper would probably be quite confusing and maybe even incorrect.

Think about this example. You are asked to write a paper about the morality of the death penalty. Before you conduct any searches on the Internet, you should determine what you will mean by "death penalty." You might believe that death by lethal injection is morally acceptable; yet you would argue that electrocution is morally unacceptable.

Suppose that you decide that in your paper you will argue that the death penalty, in the form of lethal injection only, is morally acceptable. You conduct an Internet search to find information about the death penalty and lethal injections. At "Execution Methods Used by States" (**http://www.fcc.state.fl.us/fcc/ reports/methods/emstates.html#probs**), you encounter the following information:

> As of June 15, 1997, twenty-two executions encountered problems during the execution process.

What should you do with this information? The author says that twenty-two executions encountered problems. But you don't know what kinds of executions had problems. What if *all* of these executions were by lethal injection? On the other hand, what if *none* of them was by lethal injection? You need to find out what the author means by "executions" because this information could strongly support or weaken your argument.

In summary, if you are searching for a certain definition of a word or phrase and want to rely on that information, make sure that your intended meaning matches the author's intended meaning.

Use Your Purpose as a Guide When Searching for Meaning

Now that you have learned to pay attention to multiple meanings, you have learned that you must be more careful in reading and selecting information. Your Internet search may therefore become more difficult. For example, previously you could simply type "pornography" and start reading the enormous amounts of information retrieved by the search engine. Now you must pay close attention to the potential meaning of "pornography" on each site. On the other hand, careful attention to meanings might also save you time in conducting more narrow searches for information. For example, instead of simply typing "death penalty," you could type "lethal injection."

Your purpose in searching for certain information can serve as a guide for determining meaning. For example, if you are writing a paper about the death penalty, you should determine what you mean by "death penalty" before you write the paper. In contrast, if you are attempting to arrive at an opinion about abortion, you might not want to limit your definition just yet. Instead, you might want to read numerous Web pages to see how, or if, they define "abortion" and "human life." Thus, your purpose can guide you as you search for the meanings of certain words and phrases.

Suppose that you are searching for information about exercise and its benefits for cardiovascular health because you want to make better health decisions. It would not make sense to define "exercise" narrowly. If you defined "exercise" as "walking" and searched for benefits for cardiovascular health, you might miss information suggesting that running and lifting weights provide the greatest cardiovascular benefits.

In conclusion, use the purpose of your search as a guide when searching for the meanings of unclear words and phrases. Sometimes it will help to narrowly define a key word before you search; however, be aware that a narrow definition might not be appropriate in some situations.

Chapter 8

What are the Value Assumptions?

At **http://www.fairtest.org/facts/satfact.htm** we find this information:

> The SAT consistently underpredicts the performance of females in college and overpredicts the performance of males. Although females earn higher grades in high school and college, their SAT scores were 40 points lower in 1997.

It will not take you long to find this conflicting information:

> The differences in test results between men and women will predict similar differences in other areas like grades and college achievement. These differences are not caused by innate differences between the two sexes, but test flaws do not cause them either. They are most likely caused by earlier differences in education.

How well do SAT scores reflect college achievement? Apparently, many experts disagree on this issue. Many educators feel that the SAT is highly predictive of college achievement, while others claim that the test is not predictive for certain subgroups of students. In fact, many feel that the test is biased not only against women but against all minorities.

Again, the first step in coming to a well-informed conclusion is to search for more information. Naturally, national education and testing websites will have information relevant to this issue. There may also be information on the sites of organizations that promote equal opportunity

for minorities. Here is a list of Web pages that contain information relevant to this issue:

- Association for Supervision and Curriculum Development (**http://www.ascd.org**)
- Educational Testing Service (**http://www.ets.org**)
- The Center for Individual Rights (**http://www.cir-usa.org/**)
- The Consortium for Equity in Standards and Testing (**http://wwwcsteep.bc.edu/ctest**)
- The Secrets of the SAT (**http://www.pbs.org/wgbh/pages/ frontline/shows/sats/**)

What is it that causes these experts to disagree? In this chapter we will learn that conclusions are often influenced by *value assumptions,* and that these assumptions often lead two experts to interpret the same set of facts differently. To effectively evaluate these arguments, we must be able to identify the value assumptions within them.

After studying Chapter 2, you know how to identify reasons and conclusions in an argument. You know that a conclusion is only as good as the reasons given to support it. But there is more to the structure of an argument than reasons and conclusions. Consider this example:

The grading system should not be used in college classes because students feel as if they must compete with each other instead of working and learning together.

Here is the basic structure of this argument:

Conclusion: The grading system should not be used in college classes.
Reason: The grading system is an obstacle to cooperation.

Does this argument make sense? Does the conclusion follow from the reason? At first glance the argument seems sound. The reason is correct: Grades are in fact an obstacle to cooperation. But does it follow that grades should not be used? Hidden within the argument are certain assumptions that we must accept in order to accept the argument. The author is *assuming* that cooperation is something we should strive to achieve in education. If someone felt that cooperation is of little importance in education, the argument would make no sense. The reason in this argument is true, but without the assumption, the conclusion does not *follow* from the reasoning.

An argument consists of reasons plus a conclusion, but assumptions must be added into the structure. The argument now looks something like this:

Reason

Grades prevent cooperation in education

+

Assumption

Cooperation is important

=

Conclusion

Therefore, the grading system should not be used in college classes

---

These assumptions are critical to understanding the argument, but unfortunately, most authors do not reveal them. It is *your* job to hunt for them. This can be a tricky task, but until you can identify the assumptions, you cannot have a full understanding of the argument. This chapter will help you discover assumptions by giving you tips on what to look for and where to look. Although there are many different types of assumptions, we will discuss one type in particular—*value* assumptions.

Discovering Assumptions

Before we can find these assumptions, we must have a good understanding of what they are. In general, **assumptions** have these characteristics: They are

- Hidden or unstated.
- Taken for granted.
- Influential in determining the conclusion.
- Necessary, if the reasoning is to make sense.
- Potentially deceptive.

Although all of these characteristics are important, you should pay special attention to the third one. There will be many assumptions within the websites that you find, but the only ones you should be interested in are those that are influential in determining the conclusion of the argument. It will be useful to remember that *you should look for assumptions in the movement from reasons to conclusions!*

Discovering Values

Before attempting to identify value assumptions, you need to have a clear understanding of what a value is. For the purposes of this book, we will define the word "value" as an idea that people see as worthwhile. If you recall the example at the beginning of the chapter, you will see that the author of the passage held the **value** of cooperation. She saw cooperation as an idea that was worthwhile.

Let's try to make a list of common values. (Remember that values are *ideas* that people find worthwhile. A favorite CD may be very important to you, but it is not an idea that will affect your conclusions.) It may help if you focus on ideas that are so important to you that they affect many of the decisions you make. These ideas will most likely be your values.

A second definition of values should be helpful. Think of values as standards of behavior that we endorse and expect people to meet. How do you expect the people around you to behave? Most likely, these expectations are rooted in your values.

Also, make sure your list contains only those values that most affect your behavior. Certain values have more consequences than others, and the ones that will most likely affect arguments are the only ones we need to identify in evaluating Internet sites. For example, the author of a pro-life website may value politeness, but that value will make little or no difference in her argument.

We list some commonly-held values below; perhaps that will help you think of other values for your list. When you look over the list, think about which values stand out as most and as least important in your life.

Common Values

adventure	efficiency	novelty
altruism	equality of condition	order
ambition	equality of opportunity	patriotism
autonomy	excellence	peace
collective responsibility	flexibility	rationality
comfort	freedom of speech	security
competitions	generosity	spontaneity
cooperation	harmony	tolerance
courage	honesty	tradition
creativity	justice	wisdom

Discovering Value Assumptions

Now that we have a better understanding of what a value is, we can move on to understanding value *assumptions*. As you probably noticed after generating your list, most people would include the same values on their lists. Who doesn't feel that honesty, peace, and courage are important? The issue here is not whether a person values these ideas, but rather, how *strongly* she values them. Although almost everyone values honesty, some people value it more highly than others do. Often, this difference causes two people to come to different conclusions.

Look at your list of values again. Which values do you hold more strongly than others? Are you having trouble deciding? Sometimes it is easier to determine which values we hold more strongly when we look at a situation in which two of our values conflict with each other.

For example, most of us value both competition and cooperation, but as the example at the beginning of the chapter suggests, these two values conflict with each other in certain situations. In considering the issue of the grading system, we must choose whether we *prefer* the value of cooperation or the value of competition. The *values that writers implicitly prefer over other values in certain contexts* are their value assumptions. In commenting on almost any controversial issue, the author is upholding one value while ignoring another, often without telling you. When reading an argument, ask yourself what values the author is upholding and what values he or she is ignoring. In this way you will identify the author's value assumptions.

Look for Typical Value Conflicts

It may be easier to identify the value assumptions in an argument if you have a list of typical *value conflicts*. Value conflicts occur when two values conflict with each other and a person must choose one over the other. Certain value conflicts often arise within arguments about controversial issues. To help you make a list of these typical value conflicts; we have provided you with a short list of our own:

Value Conflicts

---

rationality vs. spontaneity	tradition vs. novelty
security vs. excitement	equality vs. individualism
competition vs. cooperation	loyalty vs. honesty
freedom of speech vs. order	

Try to think of controversies in which these conflicts might arise. You already know of an issue in which the third value conflict arises, but what about the others? Where would the values of spontaneity and rationality conflict? How about, "Should you plan your vacations?" This question may sound silly, but it illustrates the point well. If you would rather go on a vacation in which everything is planned down to the last second, you prefer rationality in this instance. However, if you're the type that would rather leave for a vacation with no plan at all, you prefer spontaneity. Depending on which value you prefer, you would come to different conclusions.

Look at the Origin of the Website

An important clue to discovering value assumptions is the background of the authors. Almost anyone can create a website, and all authors have different agendas. The value assumptions of the author may be obvious if you know the author's background. For example, if you go to **http://www.aclu.org**, you will have linked to a webpage sponsored by the American Civil Liberties Union. Obviously, this is a group that tries to protect the civil liberties of Americans. This objective implies that its members value freedom over order. This value assumption is implicit within many of their arguments. You may find an argument similar to this on their website:

> Freedom of speech is crucial on college campuses. Education is about sharing opinions and ideas. Even if the ideas are harmful or offensive, they should not be restricted.

The value assumption of freedom over order is crucial to the validity of this argument. If people value order over freedom, they will not agree that all freedom of expression is important on a college campus. Sometimes freedom of expression leads to violent acts, and those who value order and security more than freedom of speech would feel that freedom of expression is not, in this instance, important on college campuses.

If we know where a website originated, it is easier to evaluate the argument because we have better ideas about the author's value assumptions. Following is a list of web sites created by organizations with particular value assumptions. This list will give you an idea of the types of value preferences different organizations may assume. (Note, however, that not every author involved in a certain group will have the same value preferences.)

Organization Web Pages and their Possible Value Assumptions

http://www.aclu.org—American Civil Liberties Union	*Freedom over Order*
http://www.madd.org—Mothers Against Drunk Driving	*Security over Freedom*
http://www.give.org—National Charities Information Bureau	*Generosity over Material Success*
http://www.essential.org—Essential Information	*Equality over Individualism*
http://www.nccbuscc.org/—National Conference of Catholic Bishops	*Tradition over Novelty*
http://www.usma.edu—United States Military Academy	*Security over Pacifism*

Look for Similar Controversies

Another trick that is often helpful in determining value assumptions is to compare the controversy underlying an argument to other similar controversies. If you make a list of controversies that are similar, it may be easier to see the value conflicts within the controversies. Let's try an example.

At **http://sen.parl.gc.ca/ckenny/itstime.htm** we find this argument:

> It's not good enough to simply tax cigarettes even higher. We tried that route. It reduced smoking somewhat but created a new problem: smuggling . . . Instead, let's cut out all cigarette advertising, promotions and sponsorships of sports and cultural events with legislation.

First, let's lay out the structure of this argument.

Issue: Should cigarette advertising be banned?
Conclusion: We should prohibit all cigarette advertising, promotions, and sponsorships with legislation.
Reason: Banning cigarette advertising will reduce smoking more than taxing cigarettes will.

Now that we have an understanding of the argument, what other issues are similar to this issue? This controversy is similar to the controversies over requiring automobile firms to include airbags in cars, requiring cyclists to wear helmets, and banning boxing. What do these issues have in common? They all fall under the more general issue, "Should collective groups intervene in people's lives to help them protect themselves?" Within this general issue we will find the value conflict underlying the argument about cigarette advertising. That value conflict is collective responsibility versus individual responsibility. If people valued individual responsibility over collective responsibility, they would not favor a ban on cigarette advertising even if it would lower the number of smokers.

Think About What is Important to Those Who Disagree

Another useful way to identify value conflicts is to ask yourself, "What would those who disagree with this website care about?" Let's try an example. While searching the Web, you find this argument about same-sex marriages:

> Same gender couples should be given the same opportunity to share in the rights, responsibilities, and commitments of a civil marriage because marriage is a basic human right.

Now, ask yourself what those who disagree with this conclusion would be most concerned about.

In many cases, those who disagree feel that allowing same-sex marriage will be violating the tradition of marriage in society. To them this concern is more important than equality. In other words, those who disagree value tradition more than they value equality in this situation. Therefore, the value conflict in this issue is between equality and tradition, and the author of the website makes the value assumption that equality should be preferred over tradition.

In summary, assumptions are hidden ideas that are influential yet are taken for granted. Value assumptions occur when an author implicitly assumes that one value should be preferred over other values in certain contexts. Looking for typical value conflicts, the author's background, similar controversies, and the values of those who disagree will provide clues to an author's value assumptions.

Chapter 9

How Good Is the Evidence?

If you were doing a study on the use of antidepressant drugs, you might come across a website with information similar to the following:

> There have been a large number of studies that prove that a new and improved antidepressant drug is actually effective, and that it is not just the placebo effect. 50 percent of the subjects in these studies responded positively to the drug, while only 32 percent of those with the placebo pill responded positively.

You may then stumble upon this conflicting information:

> An analysis of a number of studies shows that 75% of those that benefit from antidepressant drugs are simply experiencing the placebo effect. In other words, it is not the drug that is helping them; it is their psychological reaction to taking the medication. The only reason 75% of the patients benefit is that they convince themselves that the pill will benefit them.

Many people are faced with the question: Should I take antidepressant medications for my depression? They would like to know if such medications work. But such claims need to be supported by evidence. As is clear from the passages just quoted, evidence supports conflicting claims. Such conflicting evidence is widespread. A critical thinker should carefully evaluate the evidence and find out what others are saying about it. There are many kinds of evidence, and evidence rarely leads to an unambiguous conclusion about the "facts." In this chapter we help you locate evidence and judge its worth.

The Need to Evaluate Evidence

On July 17, 1996, TWA Flight 800, a Boeing 747 bound for Paris, exploded shortly after taking off from New York's Kennedy Airport, killing all 230 people on board. The National Transportation Safety Board has yet to determine the exact cause of the crash. If you were to activate a search engine on the Internet and plug in the phrase "TWA 800", you would obtain a list containing hundreds of sites dealing with the crash.

When we conducted such a search in January 2000, at **http://www.google.com/ search ?=%22TWA+800%22+AND+Causes&num=10&sa=Google+Search** we found on the initial screen (one of 40 such screens) the following sites:

INITIAL SCREEN OF SEARCH FOR INFORMATION ABOUT TWA FLIGHT 800

TWA 800 - Missile Website Roadmap

. . . TWA 800 - Missile Website Roadmap The Roadmap guides you to. . .
. . .information supporting the TWA Flight 800 Missile Theory. The. . .
www.angelfire.com/hi/TWA800/

The Fall of TWA 800: The Possibility of Electromagnetic Interference

. . .Special Supplement The Fall of TWA 800: The Possibility of. . .
. . .Reconstructing the wreckage of TWA 800 in a Long Island hangar,. . .
cryptome.org/twa800-emi.htm

ED ZEHR: TWA-800 Pitchup — The Sequel

. . . TWA-800 PITCHUP-THE SEQUEL By Ed Zehr I did a rough calculation. . .
. . .assume that this happened with TWA-800 since pilot, co-pilot and. . .
www.copi.com/articles/Goddard/ZehrGut.html

The Truth About TWA Flight 800

. . .THE TRUTH ABOUT TWA FLIGHT 800 By Reed Irvine, Chairman, Accuracy. . .
. . .NTSB's claim that the crash of TWA Flight 800 was initiated. . .
www.aim.org/special/Col980721.html

1997 SDX Awards—Investigation Uncovers Safety Problems

. . .Deeply Divided on Anniversary of TWA 800 Explosion –Battle of. . .
. . .Dissection of a Disaster—TWA Flight 800 Investigation Uncovers. . .
spj.org/sdxawards97/28/1215.htm

Click on various Web postings dealing with TWA 800. You will find many conflicting claims about the cause of the crash. Some of these claims might be *rumors* based on nothing but speculation or hearsay. Others might be based on newspaper reporters' interviews with experts, some of whom are much more knowledgeable about airplane crashes than others. Additional claims might be made by experts who had carefully studied the evidence surrounding the crash over a lengthy period. How would you decide which claims are most believable? You would need to ask: How good is the evidence?

There are hundreds of Web pages that present claims masquerading as facts. In earlier chapters we have alerted you to clues that can help you decide which sites to pay the most attention to if you want accurate information. Regardless of its reputation, however, a website can never do all your thinking for you. If you want to know whether you can rely on a claim as "the truth," you must actively check the evidence for that claim.

In this chapter you will learn to ask critical questions about a specific part of the reasoning structure: claims about the "facts." Here are a few examples of such claims:

- TWA Flight 800 was shot down by a missile.
- Infidelity is rampant in the United States.
- Binging on college campuses is increasing at an alarming rate.

What do we make of these claims? When are they legitimate? Our focus in this chapter is on the process of evaluating the accuracy of such claims by asking, "How good is the evidence?"

What is the Relationship Between "Facts" and Evidence?

Most websites present beliefs that the communicator wants us to accept as "facts." These beliefs can be opinions, conclusions, reasons, or assumptions. Let's refer to such beliefs as *factual claims*.

The first question you should ask about any factual claim is, *"Why should I believe it?"* The next question is, *"Does the claim need evidence to support it?"* Is there any reason to doubt the claim? If so, there is a need for supporting evidence. If there is no evidence, the claim is an *unsupported opinion*. You should seriously question opinions that need to be backed up by evidence but are not.

The quality of evidence varies greatly. If there is evidence, your next question is, *"How good is the evidence?"* Some factual claims can be counted on more than others. For example, you probably feel quite certain that the claim "Most CEOs in the biggest 100 corporations are men" is true, but less certain that the assertion "Parental co-sleeping with infants helps make them more secure as an adult."

We want to ask of factual claims, "Can we count on such beliefs?"—at least for the time being. The greater the quality and quantity of evidence supporting a claim, the more we can depend on it and call it a "fact." The major difference between claims that are opinions and those that are facts lies in the evidence. The more supporting evidence there is for a belief, the more "factual" the belief becomes.

Before we judge the persuasiveness of a web communication, we need to know which factual claims are most dependable. To determine dependability, we ask questions like the following:

- *What is your proof?*
- *Where's the evidence?*
- *How do you know that's true?*
- *Why do you believe that?*

Internet sites that provide good evidence for their factual claims show respect for users of their site. They communicate that they expect us to accept their claims only if they have made a convincing case for them through the use of good evidence. Sites that fail to present needed evidence treat the user as an unthinking fool rather than as a critical thinker. You should avoid such sites.

Kinds of Evidence

To evaluate evidence, we first need to ask, "What kind of evidence is it?" This tells us what further questions to ask. The most frequently used kinds of evidence are

- Appeals to authorities
- Personal testimonials

- Personal experience
- Case studies
- Research studies

Let us take a closer look at each of these. We have already addressed this topic in previous chapters. Here we just want to remind you of the frequency of this type of evidence.

Personal Testimonials and Personal Experience as Evidence

"I home-schooled my child, and now she's doing great in college."

"In only six weeks, I lost ten pounds, using Lesflab. I highly recommend it to you."

"I really enjoyed his class. You should take it."

A common strategy to support a claim is to present direct "testimonials" or "endorsements" from individuals who have had experiences related to it. Such claims are widely used in promoting books, movies, politicians, diets, medical practices, and positions on social issues such as gun control and abortion.

In most cases we should pay little attention to personal testimonials until we find out much more about the expertise, interests, values, and biases behind them. We should be especially sensitive to the following problems with testimonials:

1 *Selectivity.* People's experiences differ greatly. Those who are trying to persuade us have usually carefully selected the testimony they use. We should always ask, What was the experience like for those whom we have *not* heard from?

2. *Personal interest.* Many testimonials come from people who have something to gain from their testimony. For example, authors will sometimes provide positive testimonials for others, expecting that the favor will be returned when their book is reviewed. Always ask, Does the person providing the testimony have a relationship with what he or she is advocating such that we can expect a strong bias in his or her testimony?

3. *Omitted information.* Testimonials rarely provide sufficient information about the basis for the judgment. For example, when a friend of yours raves about a certain teacher, you should ask *why*. Our standards may differ from those of the person giving the testimony.

In general, be cautious about using either your own personal experiences or those of just a few others as evidence to support a belief. Because people differ so much, personal experiences lead us to *overgeneralize*. Single experiences can demonstrate that certain outcomes are *possible;* for example, you may have met someone who smoked three packs of cigarettes a day and lived to the age of 90. Such experiences by themselves, however, can't prove that such outcomes are *typical*.

Research Studies as Evidence

Studies show. . .

Researchers have found. . .

A recent report in the New England Journal of Medicine indicates. . .

One form of evidence that often carries special weight is the research study: a systematic collection of observations by people trained to do scientific research. How dependable are research findings? We can't tell until we ask questions.

Because the scientific method attempts to avoid many biases in our observations and in our intuition and common sense, it has a number of advantages over other methods. Above all, it seeks *publicly verifiable data*— that is, data collected under conditions such that other qualified people can make similar observations and check the results. A second major characteristic is *control:* It minimizes extraneous factors that might affect the accuracy and interpretation of claims.

While there is much more to science than we can discuss here, we want you to remember that scientific research, when conducted well, is one of the best evidence sources. Such research avoids some of the disadvantages of case studies, appeals to authority, and personal testimonials. However, it has some important limitations.

Limitations of Scientific Research

Most questions, particularly those that focus on complex human behavior, can be answered only tentatively even with the best research evidence. When communicators appeal to research as a source of evidence, you should consider these factors:

Research Varies Greatly In Quality

We should rely more on some research studies than on others. Because the research process is so complex and subject to so many external influences, even well-trained researchers sometimes conduct flawed studies; publication in a scientific journal does not guarantee that a research study is not flawed in important ways.

Research Findings Often Contradict One Another

Single research studies presented outside the context of the set of studies of the question at hand often provide misleading conclusions. Research findings that most deserve our attention are those that are presented as part of an extensive set of related findings.

Research Findings Do Not Prove Conclusions

At best, findings *support* conclusions. Researchers must always interpret their findings, and all findings can be interpreted in more than one way. Thus, researchers' conclusions should not be treated as demonstrated "truths."

Researchers are Biased

Researchers have expectations, attitudes, values, and needs that can bias the questions they ask, the way they conduct their research, and the way they interpret their findings. Despite efforts to avoid bias, science is not a neutral, value-free, totally objective enterprise. Scientists often have an emotional or financial interest in a particular hypothesis. For example, researchers who are directly funded by a major drug company may be more likely to find positive treatment results for that company's drugs than researchers who have no personal relationship with the drug company. Like all fallible human beings, researchers may find it difficult to objectively treat data that conflict with their interests.

Web Authors Often Distort or Simplify Research Conclusions

Major discrepancies may occur between the conclusion merited by the original research and the use of the evidence to support a communicator's beliefs. For example, researchers may carefully qualify their own conclusions in their original research report only to have others use the conclusions without the qualifications.

Research "Facts" Change Over Time, Especially Claims about Human Behavior

Today's "truths" are frequently disconfirmed by later research.

Research Varies in How Artifical It Is

Because of the need to control the research process, research may lose some of its "real-world" quality. The more artificial the research, the more difficult it is to generalize from the research study to the world outside. The problem of artificiality is especially evident in studies of complex social behavior. For example, to study the effects of television violence, researchers may expose children to violent cartoons and then observe how aggressive they are toward dolls. We should ask, Is aggressive behavior toward dolls too artificial to tell us much about aggressive behavior in other situations?

Questions for Evaluating Research Studies

The ability to evaluate research evidence requires an in-depth understanding of research methodologies and philosophies that this book can't provide for you. We can, however, present some questions that you can ask about research evidence.

1. What is the quality of the source of the report? Usually, the most dependable reports are those published in peer-review journals, in which a study is not accepted until it has been reviewed by a series of relevant experts. Usually—but not always—the more reputable the source, the better designed the study. So try to find out all you can about the source's reputation.

2. Other than the quality of the source, are there other clues included in the communication suggesting that the research was well done? For example, does the report detail any special strengths of the research?

3. Have conclusions from the study been supported by other findings? For example, when an association such as the link between smoking and cancer is repeatedly and consistently found in well-designed studies, there is reason to believe it, at least until those who disagree can provide persuasive evidence for their point of view.

4. How selective has the communicator been in choosing studies? For example, have relevant studies with contradictory results been omitted? Has the communicator selected only studies that support his or her point?

5. Is there any evidence of critical thinking? Has the speaker or writer shown a critical attitude toward earlier research that supports his or her point of view? Most conclusions from research need to be qualified in some way. Has the communicator demonstrated a willingness to qualify her conclusions?

6. Is there any reason for someone to have distorted the research? We need to be wary of situations in which the researchers need to find certain kinds of results.

7. Are conditions in the research artificial and therefore distorted? Always ask: How similar are the research conditions to the situation the researcher is generalizing about?

8. How far can we generalize, given the research sample? (We discuss this question in depth in the next section.)

9. Are there any biases or distortions in the surveys, questionnaires, ratings, or other measurements that the researcher uses? We need to be confident that the researcher's measurements are accurate. The problem of biased surveys and questionnaires is so pervasive that we discuss it in more detail in the next section.

Biased Surveys and Questionnaires

Surveys and questionnaires are usually used to measure people's attitudes and beliefs. Responses to them are subject to many influences; one therefore must be very cautious in interpreting their meaning. Let's examine some of these influences.

First, for survey responses to be meaningful, participants must respond honestly. What people say needs to match what they truly believe and feel. Yet individuals frequently shade the truth. For example, they may give answers that they think they ought to give, or they may experience hostility toward the questionnaire or toward the kind of question being asked. They may give too little thought to the question.

Remember: You cannot assume that survey responses accurately reflect true attitudes.

Second, the wording of many survey questions is ambiguous; the questions therefore are subject to multiple interpretations. As a result, different individuals may in effect be responding to different questions! For example, imagine the possible interpretations of the following question: "Are you happily married?" The more ambiguous the wording of a question, the less credible the results. You should always ask: How were the questions worded?

Third, questionnaires may contain many kinds of built-in biases, including biased wording and biased context. A small change in how a question is worded can have a major effect on how it is answered. Here is an example:

A U.S. congressman sent a questionnaire to his constituents and received the following results: 92 percent were against government-supported child-care centers.

Let's look closely at the survey question: "Do you believe the federal government should provide child-care centers to assist parents in rearing their children?" Do you see the bias built into the question? The "leading" words are "to assist parents in rearing their children." The responses would have been quite different if the question had read: "Do you believe the federal government should provide child-care centers to assist parents who are unable to find alternative child care while they are working?" Thus, the responses obtained by the congressman do not accurately reflect attitudes concerning child-care centers.

Other factors that influence questionnaire responses are the placement of the items relative to other items, its length, and the need to please or displease the researcher or other groups that might use the survey for their own purposes.

Some surveys are better done than others. The better its quality, the more you should be influenced by survey results. Examine survey procedures carefully before accepting survey results. Once you have ascertained the quality of the procedures, you can generate your own qualified generalization—one that takes into account any biases you might have found

For example, if the respondents in a survey are subscribers to a "liberal" magazine, you should apply any resulting generalization only to people who subscribe to that magazine. Even biased surveys can be informative; but you need to know the biases in order not to be unduly persuaded by the findings.

In summary, our focus in this chapter has been the evaluation of evidence. We have discussed four kinds of evidence: appeals to authority, testimonials, case studies, and research studies. Each kind has its strengths and weaknesses. Usually you can rely most on claims that authors support directly with extensive scientific research. However, many issues have not been settled by scientific research, and communicators therefore must rely on inconclusive research and on other kinds of evidence. You should be especially wary of claims supported by inappropriate authorities, personal testimonials, vivid case studies, or poorly designed research studies. When you encounter *any* evidence, you should try to determine its quality by asking, "*How good is the evidence?*"

Use the following Internet sites to practice in evaluating claims supported by personal observations, case studies, research studies, and analogies.

Are violent cartoons appropriate for children?

www.nonline.com/procon/html/proCV.htm

www.nonline.com/procon/html/conCV.htm

Are professional athletes overpaid?

www.nonline.com/procon/html/proSalary.htm

www.nonline.com/procon/html/conSalary.htm

Chapter 10

What Significant Information Is Omitted?

At **http://sun.soci.niu.edu/~critcrim/guns/gun.viol**, we find this information:

> Approximately 60 percent of all murder victims in the United States in 1989 (about 12,000 people) were killed with firearms. According to estimates, firearm attacks injured another 70,000 victims, some of whom were left permanently disabled. In 1985 (the latest year for which data are available), the cost of shootings—either by others, through self-inflicted wounds, or in accidents—was estimated to be more than $14 billion nationwide for medical care, long-term disability, and premature death. Among firearms, handguns are the murder weapon of choice. While handguns make up only about one-third of all firearms owned in the United States, they account for 80 percent of all murders committed with firearms.

On the other hand, the author of another website claims:

> There are numerous protective uses of guns. A recent study concluded that there are between 700,000 and 2 million protective uses of guns each year. Another study argued that there are as many as 75 lives protected by a gun for every life lost to a gun.

Are you looking for statistics to help you decide what position to take in arguments about gun control? You could find lots of them. However, the two passages just quoted indicate that you need to worry about an important problem when you use Web information in making decisions about such controversial issues. The information that you find at any particular site is selective. Other important information is almost always omitted. For example, notice that each of these passages emphasize different statistics. Had you gone to only one site, you would have been unaware of the statistics presented in the passage supporting the opposing view. We think one of the most important questions you can ask as a critical thinker is: What significant information is omitted? That question is the focus of this chapter.

The Importance of Looking for Omitted Information

How compelling are the following advertisements?

> *Most doctors prescribe Ease-Pain for headaches!*
> *Jump-Start Cola was Number 1 in recent taste tests!*

The purpose of both advertisements is, of course, to persuade you to buy more of the designated product. In such advertisements, as well as in more complex arguments, what *is not said* is often more informative than what *is said*. For example, if the Ease-Pain company gives bigger discounts to hospitals than other aspirin manufacturers do, gives hospitals more free samples, or offers cruises to physicians who use its product, this information is unlikely to be included in the ad—even though it may be highly relevant to judging the merit of the advertising claim.

By asking the questions you have learned in earlier chapters, such as those concerning the credibility of authorities and the quality of evidence, you will detect much missing information. However, your search needs to be more complete. This is an important additional question that you must ask in order to judge the quality of reasoning: What significant information is omitted? By "significant omitted information" we mean information that would affect whether you should be influenced by an author's arguments.

When you have finished this chapter, you should be familiar with three good ways to decide whether a web site has presented a good argument. The best arguments are ones that are supported by reasons that

- Are relevant to the truth of the conclusion
- Are acceptable or well supported
- Have not omitted important information

The Inevitablity of Incomplete Information

Incomplete reasoning is inevitable for several reasons. First, there are the limitations imposed by time and space. Arguments are incomplete because communicators do not have an infinite amount of time in which to organize them; and usually they do not have unlimited space or time in which to present them. Second, most of us have a limited attention span; we get bored when messages are too long. Communicators therefore often feel a need to get their message across quickly. Advertisements and editorials reflect both these factors.

Third, the communicator's knowledge is always incomplete. For example, when half the doctors sampled in a survey of attitudes toward managed care fail to complete the questionnaire, the researcher can't know whether they differ in significant ways from doctors who do complete the survey. Yet this is a very important piece of information in judging the survey's dependability.

A fourth reason information is omitted is outright attempts to deceive. Advertisers know that they are omitting key bits of information. If they were to describe all the chemicals or component parts that go into their products, you would be less likely to buy them. Experts in every field consciously omit information when open disclosure would weaken the persuasive effect of their advice. Their goal is to persuade you, not to fully inform you.

A fifth important reason is differences in values, beliefs, and attitudes. When communicators approaching an issue from one perspective, they may not be aware of other perspectives. A particular perspective is like a pair of blinders on a horse. The blinders cause the horse to focus on what is directly in front of it. Similarly, an individual's perspective may prevent him or her from noting information presented by those with differing perspectives.

Questions for Identifying Omitted Information

Because of the importance of detecting missing information, you need to remind yourself again and again to actively search for omitted information. How do you search, and what do you expect to find?

Many kinds of questions can help you identify relevant omitted information. Some of the questions you have already learned to ask will highlight important omitted information. In addition, you should always ask yourself, "Has the Web page left out any other information that I need to know before I judge the quality of its reasoning?"

Here are common kinds of significant omitted information and questions you can ask to help fill in what is missing:

- Common counterarguments

  What reasons would someone who disagrees offer?

  Are there research studies that contradict the studies presented?

  Are there missing examples, testimonials, or analogies that support the other side of the argument?

- Missing definitions

  How would the arguments differ if key terms were defined in other ways?

- Missing value preferences or perspectives

  From what other set of values might one approach this issue?

  What kinds of arguments would someone approaching the issue from a different set of values make?

- Origins of "facts" alluded to in the argument

  Where do the "facts" come from?"

  Are the factual claims supported by well-done research or by reliable sources?

- Details of procedures used for gathering facts

  How many people completed the questionnaire? Were they randomly selected? How were the survey questions worded?

  Were the participants aware of the researcher's hypothesis?

- Alternative techniques for gathering or organizing the evidence

  How might the results from an interview study differ from written questionnaire results?

- Missing or incomplete figures, graphs, tables, or data

  Would the figure look different if it included evidence from earlier or later years? Has the author "stretched" the figure to make the differences look larger?

- Omitted effects, both positive and negative, and both short-and long-term, of what is advocated and is opposed

  Has the argument left out important positive or negative consequences of a proposed action?

  Do we need to know the impact of the action in any of the following areas: political, social, economic, biological, spiritual, health, interpersonal, or environmental?

- Context of quotes and testimonials

  Has a quote or testimonial been taken out of context?

- Benefits accruing to the author from convincing others to follow her advice

  Will the author benefit financially if we adopt her proposed policy?

Let's examine an argument that has omitted some of the types of information just listed and observe how each omission might cause us to form a faulty conclusion.

Violent crime is rising in U.S. schools, according to a government survey of 10,000 students ages 12 to 19. The study, conducted by the Education and Justice departments, shows that while the overall crime rate at U.S.

schools is relatively stable, violent crime is on the rise. Comparing data from 1989 and 1995, the researchers found:

15 percent of students say they are crime victims and 4 percent say the offenses involved violence.

65 percent say they can buy drugs at school.

28 percent report gangs at school, an increase of almost 100 percent.

13 percent say they know students who bring guns to school along with their books.

It is time to pass the president's plan and spend more money on juvenile crime; we need many more prosecutors and after-school programs.

What important information do you need to know before you can decide whether to support the president's plan?

To begin with, what are possible meanings of the phrase "violent crime is on the rise"? It is not clear, for example, what is meant by "violent crime." Also, what do students mean when they say they are crime victims, and what does the phrase "involved violence" mean? "Crime victim" and "involved violence" can mean very different things to different students, and the more serious the crimes they are referring to the more concerned we are likely to be.

Are there missing or incomplete figures, graphs, tables, or data? For example, would the figures look different if they included evidence from the years between 1989 and 1995? We do not have sufficient data to determine a consistent trend. Perhaps 1995 was an atypical year. Also, what was the rate of violent crime before 1989? We could also ask whether the decreases have been greater for some groups or school settings than others, and whether that has implications for our feelings of safety. In addition, the report does not tell us how many gangs were actually *operating* in schools, only how many students were *aware* of gangs. It's possible that gangs have become more visible, which would increase student awareness.

How about the origins of the "facts" alluded to? Has the data been collected in a trustworthy fashion? Were any biases operating to influence these numbers? All of the numbers are based on self-reports of students, rather than on unbiased observations of others. Is it possible that students were more willing to report violent acts in 1995 than in 1989 because they had been sensitized to violence in the media? Also, maybe students were more willing to report the presence of gangs in 1995 than in previous years.

Are there specific value preferences or perspectives that influence the reasoning? For example, does the emphasis on government intervention as the solution keep certain other possibilities hidden, such as developing local programs that encourage greater family responsibility, or encouraging an educational campaign for children? Also, what are possible negative long-term effects of the president's plan?

Would other research methods give us a different view of the crime situation? Do we need something more than numbers of crimes? For example, would interviews with, or surveys of, people living in traditionally high-crime areas gives us a different picture of whether we're winning the war against crime? Are there events we are not measuring that we should be measuring, such as changes in the rates of parents providing after-school supervision, or changes in the numbers of children at high-risk ages? Will more kids and less control equal more crime?

As you can see, there may be an important hidden side to the findings. We have only a partial picture. Unless we complete the picture, our decisions about whether to support present crime fighting policies, or whether to feel safe in our communities, will be uninformed.

The Importance of Possible Long-Term Negative Consequences

The following argument recently appeared on several Internet sites:

> The government should require that all infants and toddlers be restrained on airplanes as they are in cars. The National Transportation Safety Board says that since 1989, at least three unrestrained children under 2 have died in plane crashes in which some passengers survived and has recommended child restraints in planes since 1990.

The goal of requiring child restraints is to make flying safer for infants. But what if such a requirement has *unintended consequences*? For example, what if such a requirement adds so much to the cost of flying that fewer parents fly and travel by car instead, and in the long run more infants are killed in car accidents than would have been killed in plane crashes?

One type of omitted information is especially important yet it is often overlooked: potential negative effects. Proposals for action are usually presented in terms of their benefits, such as greater safety, increased choice and speed, better appearance, more leisure, increased length of life, or more and/or improved commodities. However, because most actions have both positive *and* negative impacts, we need to ask several questions:

- Might the action have *unintended consequences*?
- Which segments of society do *not* benefit from a proposed action? Who loses? What do the losers have to say about it?
- How does the proposed action affect the distribution of power? Which groups gain and which groups lose?
- How does a particular action affect how we view the world: what we think, how we think, and what we know and can know?
- What effects might the action have on our health? Are there significant side effects, for example?
- How does the action affect how we relate to other people and to the environment?

66

For each of these questions, we also want to ask, "What are the potential *long-term* negative effects of the action?"

To see the usefulness of these questions, let's consider the following question: What are the negative effects of advances in computer technology? Here are some possibilities:

- *Pollution and impaired health.* For example, does computer manufacturing use large amounts of toxic materials that must eventually be disposed of at toxic dumps? Also, what is the effect of lengthy exposure to a computer terminal?
- *Shifts in employment.* How many people might lose their jobs or have to shift to less interesting jobs?
- *Invasion of privacy.* How easy will it be for others to obtain information about our incomes and habits?
- *Information acceleration.* What are the effects of information overload?
- *Military and industrial centralization.* Is it possible that with increased connections among supercomputers, some groups might gain too much power over military actions?

Questions such as these can give us pause for thought before deciding in favor of a proposed action.

Once you know what information is missing, you have a much better sense of the quality of reasoning and what you don't know that you need to know. You must now decide whether it is possible to arrive at a conclusion without the missing information.

We have pointed out that reasoning is always incomplete. Thus, to claim that you can't make a decision as long as information is missing would prevent you from ever forming any opinions. All the information you need to be absolutely certain that you are right will never be available. You need to do the best you can with the information you can obtain.

Chapter 11

Are There Rival Causes?

Recently, many newspapers reported that a recent survey of over 1500 ninth graders for 18 months found that the more TV and music videos teenagers watched, the more likely they were to start drinking alcohol. For every hour of music videos watched a day, teens' odds of starting drinking rose by about 1/3.

If you were to visit one website discussing the findings of this survey, you might find the following claim:

> This survey shows that listening to music videos and watching TV is a major cause of teen drinking. It is time that TV and music videos stop glamorizing alcohol use.

However, a visit to another site may provide you with a different interpretation of the survey results, such as the following:

> This survey indeed shows a link between time spent watching music videos and TV and teen drinking; but the findings distract us from the real causes of teen drinking – the fact that parents and peers exert a major influence on teen drinking. These kids start to watch so many videos because they are in a stage in which they want to challenge authority and they drink for the same reason.

You can find a lot of speculation about what causes teen drinking by searching the Internet. The above two passages should remind you that different websites may present contradictory ideas about such causes—even when the information they are interpreting is the same. In general, when you access the Internet for information about the causes of events of interest to you, you should check multiple sites. Experts frequently disagree on whether research has proven that a specific factor causes a particular event. Watching music videos may be an important cause of teen drinking, and it may not. As a critical thinker, you would not want to advocate for TV reform until you had carefully considered other causes.

The Need to Search for Other Possible Causes

The issue of what causes teen drinking illustrates a frequent question that we might ask from a search of websites: "What causes something to happen?" For example, we might search the Web for information to help us answer questions like the following:

> *What caused the murder rate to decrease in the United States in 1999?*
>
> *Why has the rate of depression among teenagers increased over the last 10 years?*
>
> *Does walking three times a week reduce the likelihood of heart disease?*

A common difficulty in using evidence to prove that something caused something else is the possibility of *rival causes*. The above interpretations of the survey show that the same evidence can be consistent with different interpretations. When those interpretations focus on the causes of events, we refer to them as rival causes.

Both experts and non-experts frequently emphasize one cause to explain events or research findings when other causes could also explain them. Usually, these experts will not reveal rival causes to you; you will have to identify them. Doing so can be especially helpful as you decide "how good is the evidence?" because the more plausible rival causes you can think of, the less confidence you should have in the cause proposed by the writer. Whenever you notice an author making a claim about the cause of something, always ask: Are there rival causes?

Knowing When to Look for Rival Causes

When should you look for rival causes? Whenever you notice causal thinking. As commonly used the term "cause" means "to bring about, make happen, influence, or affect." Communicators indicate causal thinking in many ways.

Following are some claims from recent articles that use language indicating the presence of causal reasoning:

- *Why* do college students drink so stupidly? *Because* drinking intelligently is against the law.
- Animal therapy *reduces* anxiety.

- Visitors *boost* their risk of heart attacks by 34 percent during their stay in New York.
- Smoking during pregnancy *fosters* violent crime.
- Marriage *brings* considerable benefits to both women and men.
- Writing about trauma *eases* illness.
- Religious attendance *improves* health.

The Pervasiveness of Rival Causes

On April 20, 1999, 13 people were killed and more than two dozen were wounded when two young men dressed in black overcoats and masks opened fire inside Columbine High School in Littleton, Colorado. The gunmen were seniors at the school and members of a student clique called the "Trenchcoat Mafia." The shootings captured the nation's attention, and Internet sites suggested many possible causes for the violent behavior.

One site dismisses many possible previously suggested causes, such as violent movies and the Internet, and instead blames "our experiences in life," citing several pieces of evidence in support of this cause, such as the fact that many Columbine athletes had treated the two teenagers badly and the that two were often called names, such as "dirtbag" and "faggot."

The results of a gallop poll are discussed at another site. In response to the poll, all of the following causes were suggested by teenagers: problems of peer relations and peer pressures, personal problems of the killers—they were sick, angry, confused, etc., ignoring of warning signals, and parental factors. In contrast, the poll found that adults mainly blamed parents and families. Other causes mentioned by adults were personal problems of the gunmen, lack of morals and religion in society, and the prevalence of violence in the media.

A third site suggests that the cause might be the current legal famework, which encourages moral mediocrity and facilitates the culture of violence that is influencing today's youth.

Now, let's leave Columbine and examine something very different in need of a causal explanation—the findings of a research study. The report is similar in form to many such reports on the Web:

A researcher reported that treating headaches with relaxation exercises and biofeedback is helpful. Three-fourths of 95 people with chronic tension headaches and about half of 75 migraine suffers studied reduced the frequency and severity of their headaches after learning how to relax head, neck, and shoulder muscles and control stress and tension with biofeedback.

In this study, the researcher probably began with the hypothesis that relaxation training causes reduction of headache suffering, and he found evidence consistent with that hypothesis. But consider some rival, or alternative, causes for the same findings:

1. Research participants were highly suggestible, and the expectation of improvement was responsible for the change; like the sugar pill placebo effect in medicine, thinking they were going to get better might have stimulated a number of physical and mental processes that caused them to feel better.
2. Participants wanted to please the researchers; they therefore reported feeling better even though they did not.
3. Most participants volunteered while undergoing highly stressful situations; they experienced a reduction in stress during the course of the study, and this reduction accounted for the reduction in symptoms.

Now, let's leave the research laboratory and turn to the sports pages.

> During the 1999 season, the frequency of home runs hit in the major leagues showed a marked increase over the average number hit during the previous five years. Manufacturers of baseballs must be doing something to liven up the ball.

The hypothesis offered by the sportswriter is that a livelier baseball, a "rabbit ball," is causing the increase in home runs. But, here are some rival causes:

1. The quality of pitching dropped markedly during the 1999 season; there were many more injuries to pitchers than usual.
2. Weather patterns were unusual during the 1999 season; the air tended to be much less humid than usual. Reduced friction resulted in greater distance for each hit.

You can find further possible causes at the following websites:

http://www.highboskage.com/HOTNEWS.HTM

http://www.highboskage.com/THEBALL.HTM

Some important lessons can be learned from the Columbine shootings, the research study, and the baseball statistics.

Lessons Learned

- Many kinds of events may have rival causes. They include clinical case studies, criminal trials, research studies, advertising statistics, sports page charts, airline crash findings, and historical events.

- Experts can examine the same evidence and identify different causes to explain it.
- Although many explanations can fit the facts some seem more plausible than others.
- Most communicators will provide only the causes they favor. The critical thinker must generate rival causes.
- Generating rival causes is a creative process; usually such causes will not be obvious.
- Even scientific researchers frequently fail to acknowledge important rival causes for their findings.
- Do not rely on a single Web page as your only source of causal hypotheses. Check out other sources.
- The certainty of a particular causal claim is inversely related to the number of plausible rival causes.

In the following sections, we explore some implications of these lessons.

Detecting Rival Causes

Locating rival causes is much like being a good detective. When you recognize situations in which rival causes are possible, you should ask questions like these:

Can I think of any other way to interpret the evidence?

What else might have caused this act or these findings?

If I looked at this from another point of view, what important causes might I see?

If this interpretation is incorrect, what other interpretation might make sense?

In the case of studies of humans, try to put yourself in the position of a participant in the study. Would you have certain expectations that would bias your behavior? Would you feel a need to please the researcher? What would it be like to complete the questionnaire or survey? If you were to behave like the research participants, what might cause you to do so?

As you try to generate rival causes, try to *blind yourself to the author's interpretation* and see whether you can construct your own. Another option is to check other websites and library resources to see whether others have responded to the research. For example, you might type in key words matching the major concepts in the study, seeking links to other sites that discuss the same issues. The more familiar you become with an issue, the easier it will be to generate rival causes.

Rival Causes and Scientific Research

An important quality of scientific research is that it uses systematic procedures to try to eliminate rival causes. That is why you see frequent reference to terms like "control groups" and "randomly assigned." In fact, certain kinds of careful research greatly limit the number of rival causes.

Human behavior, however, is very complex, and even the best research usually fails to eliminate *all* important rival causes. If that's the case, what should you do when websites use research findings to prove that one causes another? Try to find out as much as you can about the research procedures used to obtain the findings that support the hypothesis; then try to identify rival causes that might explain the findings. The more plausible rival causes there are, the less faith you should have in the hypothesis favored by the communicator.

Confusing Causation With Association

We have an inherent tendency to "see" events that are associated, or "go together," as events that cause one another. That is, we conclude that because characteristic X (e.g., early childhood abuse) is *associated* with characteristic Y (e.g., having an eating disorder), X causes Y.

When we think this way, however, we are often very wrong! Usually, the tendency of the condition of X and the condition of Y to "go together" can be explained in several different ways. Consider an example:

A recent study reported that "hostility hurts women's health." The researchers studied women over a 31-year period and found that those who were high in hostility at ages 21, 27, and 43 experienced more illness at age 52 than women who were low in hostility. Illness included everything from colds to serious illness. The researchers hypothesized that anger may release stress hormones or impair immunity.

Should women who are high in hostility worry about their physical health? Not yet. First they should consider four potential explanations for the research findings.

> *Explanation 1:* X is a cause of Y. (Hostility does indeed impair women's health; perhaps it stresses their immune system.)
>
> *Explanation 2:* Y is a cause of X. (Being in poor health may make women feel hostile.)
>
> *Explanation 3:* X and Y are associated because of a third factor, Z. (Perhaps both hostility and poor health are caused by poor health-related behaviors, such as smoking and lack of exercise, or by stressful life events.)
>
> *Explanation 4:* X and Y influence each other. (Perhaps feeling hostile weakens one's immune system, and in turn, a weaker immune system makes one feel tired, and this makes one feel more hostile.)

Remember: Association or correlation does not prove causation! When an author relies on an association between characteristics to support a particular explanations, always ask, "Are there other causes that explain the association?"

Explaining Specific Events or Acts

Why did President Clinton become sexually involved with a White House intern? What caused the downfall of the Dallas Cowboys in 1999? What caused the stock market to grow far beyond the experts' expectations in 1999?

Like our question about reasons for the Columbine killings, these questions seek the causes of a particular event. Thus far, scientific research has not uncovered general laws powerful enough to explain such specific events. Instead, those seeking understanding frequently search the past for clues. For several reasons, such a search makes us highly susceptible to errors of reasoning. Several of these reasons are especially important to remember.

First, as we saw in the Columbine situation, so many different explanations for the same event can "make sense." Second, how we explain events is greatly influenced by social and political forces, as well as by individual psychological forces. For example, liberals might view the causes of homosexuality differently than conservatives, and feminists might view the causes of anorexia much differently than physicians.

Also, a common bias is the *fundamental attribution error,* in which we overestimate the importance of personality traits relative to situational factors in interpreting the behavior of others. We tend to see the cause of other people's behavior as coming from inside (their personal characteristics) rather than from outside (situational forces.) So, for example, when someone shows up late for a date, we're likely to initially view the lateness as being due to the person's tendency to procrastinate or be inconsiderate. However, we should also consider the role of unforeseen situational circumstances, such as car trouble, heavy traffic, or unanticipated company. Consider how differently you would consider the causes of the Columbine shootings if you believed that such acts were usually the result of situational factors than if you believed that they were caused by some kind of evil inside of the person.

Evaluating Rival Causes

The more plausible the rival causes that you identify, the less faith you can have in the initial cause suggested, at least until you can consider further evidence. As a critical thinker, you should assess how each explanation fits the available evidence as well as other knowledge you are aware of, trying to be sensitive to your personal biases. You need to be particularly suspicious when the *only* evidence backing up a cause is post hoc (after the fact) reasoning. We encourage you to add to your list of possible causes by checking multiple Internet sites whose authors are likely to differ in values, perspectives, and political orientations. Then try to determine which of these causes best fits the evidence.

Use the following Internet sites to practice finding rival causes.

Does tabloid journalism have negative effects on society?

www.nonline.com/procon/html/proTJ.htm

www.nonline.com/procon/html/conTJ.htm

What is the relationship between violent television programming and crime?

www.nonline.com/ProCon/html/proTV.htm

www.nonline.com/ProCon/html/conTV.htm

Chapter 12

Anthropology and the Internet

The Contestable Nature of Research

Whenever you conduct anthropological research on the Internet, you will encounter a variety of conflicting claims. For example, while you are searching for theories of female infanticide in foraging, agricultural, and horticultural societies, you might find one Web page where the author argues that infanticide occurs because women do not hunt to support the group. In other words, girls are viewed as being of less worth because they only gather vegetables and do not provide protein to the group. Furthermore, the practice of female infanticide led to a shortage of women that then gave rise to the practices of bride capture and fraternal polyandry.

Another point of view, more sociological in nature, is that female infanticide is gender violence and is deeply entrenched in almost all cultures. Various forms of gender violence occur, including discriminatory treatment by the family as well as the state, discrimination in health care, education, access to food, rights to resources, and in extreme forms such as female infanticide and feticide.

However, when you continue your research on another Web page, you are surprised to discover that yet another author suggests a very different reason for female infanticide. This author argues that females suffer because of the interplay between nutrition and population; in other words, pre-technological populations must be controlled and this is accomplished through the use of female malnutrition, crude abortion techniques, and infanticide.

Clearly, these authors disagree about the reasons for female infanticide. One argues that female infanticide is the result of gender violence, another argues that female infanticide is simply a population control technique, while yet another states that female infanticide occurs because women do not hunt.

Which author should we believe? Why do these authors offer conflicting viewpoints? When anthropologists conduct research studies, they have to interpret their findings. The anthropologist's perspectives, values, assumptions, and beliefs influence these interpretations. Furthermore, anthropologists belong to formal "schools" (theoretical models of behavior), or what Marvin Harris calls research strategies. Therefore, one explanation for the conflicting viewpoints about female infanticide is that the anthropologists who conducted the research had different perspectives, values, assumptions, beliefs, and, maybe more importantly, theoretical backgrounds. But what should *you* do when you encounter these conflicting claims?

Should you continue searching until you find the RIGHT page about female infanticide? If you searched until you found the RIGHT page, you would never stop searching. Remember, different perspectives, values, assumptions, beliefs, and theories shape information. Thus, there is rarely one "right" answer. Instead of looking for someone to give you the right answer, you need to evaluate the information you read and decide which claims seem the most credible.

Because searching for the RIGHT page is futile, you should examine multiple pages when conducting your Internet research. Why? Perhaps on your first search, you retrieved the Web page written by the second author, who believes that female infanticide is due to gender violence. If you did not conduct any other searches or retrieve any other Web pages, you might use this information without knowing that others have alternative theories to explain female infanticide. Consequently, it could be dangerous to rely on just one Web page for your research.

In conclusion, remember that when you search for anthropological information on the Internet, you will likely encounter conflicting claims. You should view this conflicting information as a positive aspect of the Internet. Instead of simply relying on one author's argument, you can consider several arguments and choose the conclusion that you think is the strongest.

Websites on Female Infanticide

1. http://www.unrisd.org/html/op/opb/opb7/op705.htm
2. http://www.voicenet.com/~nancymc/marvinharris.html
3. http://www.as.ua.edu/ant/Faculty/murphy/evol.htm

What are Important Websites for Anthropology Students?

If you have ever typed the word "Anthropology" into a search engine, you know that there are thousands of anthropological websites on the Internet. These websites may range from collections of anthropology sites to addressing a single issue in anthropology.

As an anthropology student, you might want to look at *Let's Go Anthropology: Travels on the Internet (1998)*. This book was created as a guide to help students navigate the Internet to conduct anthropological research. Because the book is arranged by specific areas within anthropology, it is especially effective at demonstrating the wide variety of anthropological sites available on the Internet.

While anthropologists have noted the beneficial aspects of using the Internet for research and teaching purposes, they have also said that perhaps the biggest problem associated with student Internet use is that students do not evaluate the websites they encounter. However, if you have read the previous chapters of this book, you have learned a series of evaluative questions that will help you determine the worth of information presented on a website. After reviewing the websites available to you, you will learn to use these critical-thinking questions in the context of evaluating anthropology websites.

Websites for Using the Internet

Internet Starter Kit (Macmillan Computer Publishing)	http://www.mcp.com/resources/geninternet/
Web Resources	http://www.w3.org
World Wide Web FAQ	http://sunsite.unc.edu/boutell/faq/faq.txt
Learn the Net	http://www.learnthenet.com/english/index.html
Understanding and Using the Internet	http://www2.pbs.org/uti/
Newbie Training	http://www.newbie.net/CyberCourse
The Internet for Social Scientists	http://www.unesco.org/most/brochur3.htm
Interactive Guide to the Internet	http://www.sierramm.com/smpnet.html
Evaluating Internet Resources	http://www.albany.edu/library/internet/evaluate.html
Evaluating Quality on the Net	http://www.tiac.net/users/hope/findqual.htmi

Digital Library Websites

Gateway to Europe's National Libraries	http://portico.bl.uk/gabriel/
Worldwide Digital Library Research Projects	http://www.dlib.org/projects.html#national
Digital Library Initiative (Social Science Team)	http://anshar.grainger.uiuc.edu/dlisoc/ socsci-site/index.html
University of California at Berkeley	http://elib.cs.berkeley.edu/
University of Michigan	http://www.si.umich.edu/UMDL
University of Illinois	http://dli.grainger.uiuc.edu
University of California at Santa Barbara	http://alexandria.sdc.ucsb.edu/
Carnegie Mellon University	http://www.informedia.cs-cmu.edu
Library of Congress Digital Library	http://@www.loc.gov/
Berkeley Digital Library SunSITE	http://sunsite.berkeley.edu/
Humanities Texts	http://english-server.hss.cmu.edu
elib Homepage	http://ukoin.bath.ac.uk/elib/
The Electric Library	http://www.elibrary.com/
The Electronic Newsstand	http://www.enews.com

General Websites for Humanities and Social Sciences

The HUMBUL Gateway: International Resources for the Humanities	http://users.ox.ac.uk/-humbul/
Humanities HUB: Selected Resources for the Social Sciences and Humanities	http://www.gu.edu.au/gwis/hub/
TradeWave Galaxy: Humanities/Social Sciences Indices	http://www.einet.net
Social Science Indices	http://www.osu.edu/units/sociology/indices.htm
Coombsweb Social Sciences Server	http://coombs.anu.edu.au/

INFOMINE for the Social Sciences, Humanities, and the Arts	http://lib-www.ucr.edu/liberal/
The Argus Clearinghouse: Arts and Humanities/Social Sciences and Social Issues	http://www.clearinghouse.net/index.htmi
The WWW Virtual Library	http://vlib.stanford.edu/Overview.html
Voice of the Shuttle Guide to the Humanities and Social Sciences	http://humanitas.ucsb.edu/
H-Net: Humanities and Social Sciences Online Home Page	http://h-net.msu.edu/
Social Science Information Gateway	http://sosig.ac.uk/
Forum on Technology, Media and Society	http://tunisia.sdc.ucsb.edu/speed/

Some Examples of Anthropology-related Websites

The Liebhaber Lab	http://hughes.humgen.upenn.edu/Iiebhaberlab/
Latest research in the field of anthropology	http://www.usc.edu/dept/raiders/story/fini.html
Dictionaries covering some 130 different languages	http://www.bucknell.edu/-rbeard/diction.html
The World of Language	http://www.worldoflanguage.com/uage
The Human Languages	http://www.june29.com/HLP/
Languages of Malawi	http://www.sil.org/ethnologue/countries/Mala.html
Anthropological News and Events	http://www.tamu.edu/anthropology/news.html
The UCLA Fowler Museum of Cultural History	http://www.fmch.ucla.edu/
Fossil Hominids	http://www.talkorigins.org/faqs/fossil-hominids.html
Ambling Australopithecine	http://www.discover.com/search/index.htmi
Hominid paleo-ethology	http://www.ub.es/SERP/EtoHom/indexE.html
Food and Agriculture Organization	http://www.fao.org
The Polygamy Page	http://www.familyman.u-net.com/polygamy.html
Alaskan Yupik Eskimo	http://www.adobe-east.com/Alaska-l.html
The Monkey Room	http://users.nye.net/-macaquehruthintro.htm
Creature of the Dark	http://artsci.wustl.edu/-kabiela/
Primate Conservation in Vietnam	http://coombs.anu.edu.au/-vern/iebr.htmi
Golden Spider Monkey	http://www.birminghamzoo.com/ao/mammal/ghspider.htm
Vocalization of Monkeys	http://www.selu.com/~bio/PrimateGallery/sound/index.html
Tattoo	http://miavxl.muohio.edu/-taylorw1/
Javanese Mask Collection	http://www.fmnh.org./exhibits/javamask/javamask.htm
Palaeolithic Figurines	http://www.civilization.ca/membrs/archaeo/paleofig/pal00eng.html
The Center for Genetic Anthropology	http://www.ucl.ac.uk/tcga/
The Fossil Evidence for Human Evolution in China	http://www.cruzio.com/~cscp/index.htm
Prominent Hominid Fossils	http://www.talkorigins.org/faqs/homs/specimen.html
Prosimian Primates	http://www.duke.edu/web/primate/psimians.html
Ape Ancestors	http://www.mytownnet.com/content/WA/Aberdeen/Gigantopithecus.htm

Street Gangs in Los Angeles	http://www.csun.edu/-hcchsOO6/gang.html
BURN! Social Change and Cultural Democracy	http://burn.ucsd.edu/
Economic Anthropology	http://www.lawrence.edu/-peregrip/seahome.html
Introduction to the Marquesas	http://www2.hawaii.edu/-mcarson/introduction.html
Social Stratification and Social Mobility	http://risya3.hus.osaka-u.ac.jp/shigeto/ssm/ssmE.html
The Bilateral Kindred	http://www.umanitoba.ca/anthropology/tutor/fundamentals/bilat.html
The Child/Adolescent Psychoanalysis	http://www.westnet.com/-pbrand/
Kinship and Social Organization	http://www.umanitoba.ca/anthropology/kintitle.html

Anthropology-related Journals and Newsletters

Aerial Archaeology Newsletter	http://www.nmia.com/-jaybird/AANewsletter/
African Archaeology Review	http://www.plenum.com
American Antiquity	http://www.saa.org/Publications/AmAntiq/amantiq.htmi
AnthroGlobe	http://www.webzines-vancouver.bc.ca/AnthroGlobe/
Anthropoetics	http://www.humnet.ucla.edu/humnet/anthropoetics/home.html
Anthropological Review	http://wings.buffalo.edu/anthropology/A]FtD
Anthropology Today	http://lucy.ukc.ac.uk/rai/
Archaeological Computing Newsletter	http://www.gla.ac.uk/Acad/Archaeology/acn/acn.html
Archaeology Magazine	http://www.he.net/-archaeol/index.html
Berkeley Archaeology	http://www.qal.berkeley.edu/arf/
British Archaeology	http://britac3.britac.ac.uk/cba/ba/ba.html
Bulletin of Information on Computing in Anthropology	http://lucy.ukc.ac.uk/bicaindex.html
Chicago Anthropology Exchange	http://www.lib.uchicago.edu/LiblnfoSourcesBySubject/Anthropology/CAE/
Critique of Anthropology	http://www.sagepub.co.uk/joumals/usdetails/jOO40.html
Cultural Anthropology	http://www.pitzer.edu/-cultanth
Cultural Anthropology Methods	http://www.lawrence.edu/-bradleyc/cam.html
Current Anthropology	http://www.artsci.wustl.edu/-anthro/ca
Current Archaeology	http://www.archaeology.co.uk
Discover Archaeology	http://www.discoverarchaeology.com
Ethnomusicology Online	http://www.research.umbc.edu/eol/eol.html
The Glyph	http://www.web-sculptors.com/glyph/open.htmi
Human Organization	http://www.smu.edu/-anthrop/humanorg.htmi
Internet Archaeology	http://intarch.york.ac.uk
Journal of Field Archaeology	http://jfa-www.bu.edu
Journal of Material Culture	http://www.sagepub.co.uk/journals/usdetails/j0101.html
Journal of Roman Archaeology	http://www.journalofromanarch.com/
Journal of the Royal Anthropological Institute	http://Iucy.ukc.ac.uk/rai/jrai.html
Journal of World Anthropology	http://wings.buffalo.edu/academic/department/anthropology/jwa

Journal of World-Systems Research	http://csf.colorado.edu/wsystems/jwsr.html
Midcontinental Journal of Archaeology	http://www.uiowa.edu/~osa/publica/mcja/meja.htm
Music & Anthropology	http://gotan.cirfid.unibo.it/M&A/M&A-main.htm
Northeast Anthropology	http://www.albany.edu/northeast-anthropology/
Online Archaeology	http://avebury.arch.soton.ac.uk/journal/joumal.html
Radiocarbon	http://packrat.aml.arizona.edu
Society for American Archaeology	http://www.sscf.ucsb.edu/SAABulletin
Theoretical Anthropology	http://www.univie.ac.at/voelkerkunde/theoretical-anthropology/
World Heritage Center Newsletter	http://www.unesco.org/whc/news/index-en.htm

Anthropology-related Societies

American Anthropological Association	http://www.atneranthassn.org/
American Ethnological Society	http://www.princeton.edu/-emartin/aes/
Association for Feminist Anthropology	http://members.aol.com/afeminista/afa/
Association of Latina and Latino Anthropologists	http://www.monterey.edu/academic/centers/sbsc/ALLA/index.html
Association for Political and Legal Anthropology	http://apla.sbc.edu/apla/
Society for American Archaeology	http://www.saa.org/
Society for Anthropology in Community Colleges	http://www.ccanthro.org/
Society for the Anthropology of Europe	http://www.h-net.msu.edu/-sae/
Society for Applied Anthropology	http://www.telepath.com/sfaa/
Society for Latin American Anthropology	http://www.ucr.edu/anthro/slaa/Slaa I.htm
Society for Medical Anthropology	http://www.people.memphis.edu/-sma/
Society for Visual Anthropology	http://custwww.xensei.com/docued/sva/

Anthropology-related Newsgroups

sci.anthropology
sci. anthropology.paleo
sci.archaeology
sci.archaeology.mesoamerican
sci.archaeology. moderated
sci.lan
soc.misc
soc.culture

Anthropology-related Discussion Groups

ABA-SIG	Black Anthropologists Interest Group:	**listproc@mcfeelevcc.utexas.edu**
ACRA-L	American Cultural Resources Association:	**listproc@listproc.nonprofit.net**
ADS-ALL	Digital Archiving of Archaeological Data:	**mailbase@mailbase.ac.uk**
AEGEANET	Pre-Classical Aegean World:	**majordomo@acpub.duke.edu**

AIA-L	Archaeology & Technology: **majordomo@brynmawredu**
ANSS-L	Anthropology, Sociology and Related Specialists: **listserv@uci.edu**
ANTHEURASIA-L	Anthropology of Eurasia: **majordomo@fas.harvard.edu**
ANTHRO-L	General Anthropology: **listserv@listservacsu.buffalo.edu**
ANTHROWOMEN	Women Anthropologists: **majordomo@list.pitt.edu**
ANTHTHEORY-L	Theoretical Anthropology: **listserv@list.nih.gov**
ANT-ARQ	South American Anthropology and Archaeology: **majordomo@ccc.uba.ar**
APLA-L	Political and Legal Anthropology: **majordomo@virginia.edu**
ARCH-DE	German Archaeology: **majordomoC&charon.ufg.uni-freiburg.de**
ARCH-L	General Archaeology: **listserv@listservtamu.edu**
ARCHCOMP-L	Computing in Archaeology: **listserv@listservacsu.buffalo.edu**
ARCHPUB	Archaeological Publications: **majordomo@mail.serve.com**
BRITARCH	British Archaeology: **mailbase@mailbase.ac.uk**
C 14-L	Carbon Dating: **listserv@listservarizona.edu**
CAE-L	Council on Anthropology and Education: **listproc@lmrinet.ucsb.edu**
CERAMICS-L	Prehistoric Ceramics: **listserv@listservacsu.buffalo.edu**
CONSDIST	Cultural Materials: **consdist-request@lindystanford.edu**
DEVEL-L	Technology and Development: **listserv@american.edu**
EASIANTH	Anthropology of East Asia: **listserv@vm.temple.edu**
ETHMUS-L	Ethnomusicology: **listserv@umdd.umd.edu**
FOLKLORE	Folklore: **listserv@tamvml.tamu.edu**
GISARCH	Archaeology and GIS: **mailbase@mailbase.ac.uk**
H-SAE	Society for the Anthropology of Europe: **listserv@msu.edu**
HUMEVO-L	Human Evolutionary Research: **listserv@freya.cc.pdx.edu**
LINGUIST	Discussion on Linguistics: **listserv@tamvml.tamu.edu**
MUSEUM-L	Issues related to Museums: **listserv@home.ease.Isoft.com**
PAN-L	Physical Anthropology: **listserv@freya.cc.pdx.edu**
SOLGA-L	Society of Lesbian and Gay Anthropologists Listserv: **listserv@american.edu**
SUB-ARCH	Marine Archaeology: **listserv@asuvm.inre.asu.edu**
WOMANTH-L	Women in anthropology: **listserver@relaydoit.wisc.edu**

Searching for the Right Search Engine

When you're searching for information, if you aren't sure where to start, a good place is usually a search engine of some kind. What you find will depend on the particular search engine, so it is helpful to understand the range of search tools available. Categories of search tools include: hierarchical indexes, standard search engines, alternative search engines, meta search engines, and databases. In a hierarchical index, people trained to categorize information, such as librarians, examine websites and put them in categories and subcategories. Such categorizing makes it easier for you to find relevant sites; for example, if you browse within Alpha Search, **http://www.calvin.edu/library/searreso/internet/as/**, you will find a category called "Gateways-Social Sciences," and under that category you will find anthropology subcategories. Several other useful hierarchical indexes are:

Yahoo, **http://www.yahoo.com**, BUBL Link, **http://www.bubl.ac.uk/link**, and Infomine, **http://infomine.ucr.edu**.

Unlike hierarchical indexes, standard search engines send out "robots" or "spiders" to search the Web and index the pages in each site they encounter. Each engine then uses some system to rank pages, such as calculating the frequency and placement of your keywords on a page. The search engine puts the pages that get the highest score at the top of the list of results. It is usually best to avoid standard search engines when you have a very broad subject, such as "violence" or "gender," and instead focus on a few relevant sites from a hierarchical index. Standard search engines include: AltaVista, **http://www.altavista.com**, Excite, **http://www.excite.com**, Go Network **http://infoseek.go.com**, and HotBot, **http://hotbot.lycos.com**.

Alternative search engines try to improve the search process over standard engines by using different approaches to the ranking and sorting of the pages. Northern Light, **http://www.northernlight.com**, for instance, ranks Web pages as a standard search engine does, but rather than displaying all findings in a single listing, it sorts pages into categories and groups the results into folders. For example, a search for "marriage and divorce" creates 12 folders, with names such as: "Search Current News," "Special Collection Documents," "Divorce," "Adultery," and "Divorce Law." Such arrangement of material can help you determine which groups of pages are most likely to be relevant to your needs. Another alternative engine, Google, **http://www.google.com**, first matches up your keywords to the pages it has collected in its index, then ranks each page based on how many other pages link to it—and how many links to those pages in turn. Thus, it puts pages with the most links at the top of its list.

Oingo, **http://www.oingo.com**, conducts a "conceptual search" to make sure that it understands your request. Ask it to search for "family violence," for example, and it will ask you if you want to search under the phrase "domestic violence." Then, Oingo will display "directory hits" and "Web hits." Under "directory hits," for example, you will see "Domestic Violence" and "Dating Violence," and under "Web hits," you will see such sites as "The Family Violence Prevention Fund" and "Parentbooks—Child Abuse/Domestic Violence." The site combines a hierarchical index and a search engine.

Search engines that search other engines are called meta search engines. Several popular ones are Dogpile, **http://www.dogpile.com**, Inference Find, **http://www.inferencefind.com**, and MetaCrawler, **http://www.metacrawler.com**. The underlying rationale is that no single search engine can scan all sites. A drawback to these sites is that they need to use search strategies that can be followed by all of the search engines; thus, they're usually not the best choice for complex searches.

The above search tools will eventually get you to most of the discipline-specific sites that we previously mentioned. Regardless of how you choose to search for information, you will get the best results if you know what information you need and become familiar with the advantages and disadvantages of different kinds of searches.

Thinking Critically About Anthropological Information on the Internet

In this section, we apply the critical-thinking questions that the book has been emphasizing by critically evaluating some information from the discipline of anthropology. The purpose of this discussion is to provide a brief example of a coherent application of the diverse critical-thinking steps. We suggest that you use this discussion as a check on your understanding of the previous chapters. Would you have asked the same questions? Would you have formed similar questions? Do you feel better able to judge the worth of someone's reasoning?

Critical Thinking Questions Checklist:

1. What argument does the site make?
2. How dependable is the authority providing the information?
3. What ambiguity is contained in the information?
4. What values does the site reflect?
5. How good is the evidence for the information?
6. What are the rival causes for the information?
7. What significant information is omitted?

Suppose you are writing a paper on new finds in Egyptian archaeology and are attracted by a television program on the subject that also is linked to a website. The website address is: **http://foxnews.com/fn99/science/egypt/main_post.sml**. Here is the major information presented on the website:

1. The secrets of ancient Egypt are revealed for the first time on live television.
2. The Egyptian government's chief archaeologist, Dr. Zahi Hawass, pried open the stone coffins of a man and a small child, revealing well preserved, mummified remains, while a third sarcophagus belonging to the governor of Bahariya yielded only dust, a few bones, and a collection of small statues and amulets that had been placed alongside the dead official to assist him in the afterlife.
3. The authors of the website compare this televised spectacle to a popular European parlor practice of British, French, and Italian 19th-century treasure hunters. In the past, mummies would be excavated in Egypt, shipped to Europe, and opened in front of dinner guests as an evening's entertainment.
4. Related stories are provided to show how this television program and website relate to overall Egyptian history.
5. Background information on Dr. Zahi Hawass and Egyptian history is supplied to the reader who takes time to review it. Most of this was not available in the televised version of the program.
6. A map of Egypt showing the Bahariya Oasis is available.

Let's go though the process of applying the critical-thinking questions to this website.

What argument does the site present?

Remember, when you first encounter a website, you want to make sure you understand what the author is trying to make you believe. Thus, you should think to yourself, "What is the author's main point? What is the author's purpose in creating this website?"

The authors created this site to supplement a live television program. The live program was mostly showmanship with little scientific context. The site was created to present material to people whose curiosity was piqued by the live broadcast. As this was a television broadcast for the lay public, little or no scientific argument is presented. There is no anthropological background supplied with this material. Basically, the site presents a simplified historical view of the material.

How dependable is the authority that provided the information?

This page tells us nothing about the people who created the page. We can assume that since this site was created for a large commercial television network it was created for entertainment rather than scholarly research. The one scholar involved in this event, Dr. Zahi Hawass, is obviously quite credible, but how much control he had over the material presented to the public is in question.

What ambiguity is contained in the information?

We need to know more about the Greco-Roman period of ancient Egypt to evaluate the information presented in this site. One related story gives a very brief outline of the Greco-Roman period that began with the conquest of Egypt by Alexander the Great in 332 B.C. One interesting conclusion to this short article is that it appears that mummification became much more prevalent in this period. Why this is the case is not even hypothesized here.

What values does the site reflect?

Unfortunately, this site seems to reflect the sensationalism of archaeology, commonly depicted in movies, television, and fiction. Very little of the scientific perspective of modern archaeology is shared with the public. It appears that rather than explaining the scientific and historical significance of this excavation, the public need for entertainment is exploited so as to raise funds for both the television network and further archaeological work in Egypt.

How good is the evidence for the information?

In answering this question, you want to first ask, "What is the evidence?" You need to identify the type of evidence that the authors provide. In the case of this site and its related television broadcast, the evidence for these Greco-Roman period mummies of Bahariya is quite good. The one archaeological authority, Dr. Hawass, is quite reputable. His biography is presented on this site. On a different level, the question of how the time period was determined is left mostly to the imagination of the audience and readers. Other than the interpretation of a few hieroglyphics, the chronological evidence is missing.

What are the rival causes for the information?

The authors do not make any causal claims. Instead, Dr. Hawass states "the tomb's archaeological significance lies in its vivid depiction of the governor's times, when the kingdom's Libyan rulers imitated the styles of Egypt's most celebrated periods." Rather than explaining the scientific questions that underlie the archaeological work presented here historical arguments are presented.

What significant omitted information is there?

The information omitted is much more than that submitted to the website viewer. No theoretical orientation (school of thought or research strategy) is presented. Scientific questions that would devolve from a particular research strategy are also missing. While the background information helps place the significance of this archaeological work in historical perspective, even that could be better detailed.

Conclusion

Your use of critical-thinking questions has demonstrated the weaknesses of this website for student use in an archaeology research paper or class. Both the television program and the website are flawed from a purely scientific viewpoint. While history is an important element of this website, it is clear that sensationalism is the goal.

From the standpoint of a serious student, this website would be of little use other than as a lead-in to serious research. Once exposed to this material, the serious student can go on to further research to validate the material presented and to find the scientific explanations for some of the more interesting points presented on the website, such as why mummification became more popular and prevalent during this time period, how the transition from the earlier Dynastic periods to Libyan rule affected the daily life of the Egyptian people, and how the Greco-Roman period eventually led to the end of mummification.

While this website may seem to be a crass commercialization of archaeology, it should also be noted that by preparing sites like this the public's interest in archaeology is encouraged and funding for serious research may continue. But as a research tool this website can only stand as the briefest of introductions to a very serious archaeological subject.

Appendix A

A Unique Online Study Resource: The Companion Website

This last chapter will describe a few of the textbook-specific Internet resources that are available to you and will suggest some ideas about on-line education. Hopefully, you will see a glimmer of the future of information, education, and books through your experience with these resources. Your textbook now includes an added digital tool chest, an alter-ego if you will, called a Companion Web (CW). It contains many tools to help you visualize, communicate, and discover concepts introduced in your paper textbook.

A Web Companion

The obvious question is "How do I find the CW site that goes with my book?" Fortunately, there is an easy answer to this question. All Prentice Hall textbooks have a convention for addressing their CW sites. The last name of the first author of the textbook is used to distinguish one site from another. If you add the authors last name to the standard Prentice Hall Web address (**http://www.prenhall.com/**), then you will find the CW for his book. For example:

http://www.prenhall.com/troyka/

In this fashion, you should be able to find a CW for any book if you know the author. Because you might not know the author for a book on every subject you'll want, there is an indirect way to reach all of the CW sites. Simply load the Prentice Hall home page (**http://www.prenhall.com/**) and select the Companion Website Gallery option from the page. All of the Prentice Hall CW sites are organized by discipline and are available from the CW Gallery.

Here is a partial list of science CW addresses to give you a perspective of the breadth of resources available to you.

Science Topic	Web Address
Sociology	**http://www.prenhall.com/macionis/**
Psychology	**http://www.prenhall.com/morris/**
English	**http://www.prenhall.com/troyka/**
Political Science	**http://www.prenhall.com/burns/**
History	**http://www.prenhall.com/faragher/**

There are CW sites that support every major discipline that you'll encounter in college. In addition, if your professor is not using a book with a CW site, then you can always browse through the CW Gallery until you find a resource to help you with any topic.

Now that you know where you can find your CW, here's what you'll see when you look inside. Just as a tool box is a container for tools, so too your CW is a container for unique Web tools. All CW's share a few basic tools accessible from the first page of their site. The CW site for Peter Stiling's Ecology textbook is a good example. In addition to an image of the textbook, you will find the following three features.

Syllabus Manager

This tool both allows your professor to create and manage an on-line syllabus for your course *and* enables you to view the syllabus as part of your CW. This tool is valuable to you only if your professor first develops an on-line syllabus with it. If they haven't but you think that it would be helpful, then you might consider offering to help them. You can learn more about this tool by taking the Syllabus Creation Walk-Thru found on the Syllabus Manager page.

An on-line syllabus will enable you to reach assigned activities within the CW site, sites for assignments outside the CW, and your professors individual Web pages. If your professor already has an on-line syllabus in the Syllabus Manager tool then you only need to find it to use it. To do this, simply use the search selector on the Syllabus Manager page, type in your professor's name or your college, and select the "Search Now" button. A list of on-line syllabi will be displayed from which you can select your course. Once you select your course, a calendar will appear in the lower left corner of the browser page. This calendar will contain dates and assignments as posted by your professor. It's actually fairly easy to use, but if you need more help you can select the Help tool also found on the front page of every CW site. We'll explain more about this later.

There is another scenario. If you are using a computer in a campus lab, you may occasionally find that other students will leave a syllabus loaded when you sit down to use the computer. The last option at the bottom of the syllabus calendar will unload the last syllabus and return you to the menu where you can select your own syllabus. Additionally, even if you sit down to a computer without a loaded syllabus, within the syllabus request window, you may see a list of syllabi for other courses and professors. If you've already used this tool, you might even find that your course is included in this list. You have the option of selecting your course from the list or searching for it again.

Your Profile

This tool is intended to help make your use of the CW resources more rewarding. The information that you enter into this tool is used to help you customize your experience with the CW site. Once this information is entered, when you come back to this site, some of the basic features will be preset and ready for your use. As we mentioned earlier, be aware of the situation where someone else might use information you preset or where you might use information they preset in a shared computer. If you do share a computer, then you should probably skip over this tool.

Help

It's all in the name. If you are having a difficult time using one of the chapter tools, configuring your browser, or using the Syllabus Manager, then you can find help here. Probably the most helpful of the resources you'll find in Help is called the Browser Tune-Up. It is a resource that will diagnose your browser and its plugins to determine if you have the latest versions of the software. If you do not have the latest versions, you can download them through the tool and test them to make sure they are working properly. It will probably be helpful to do this on a periodic basis in the event a new version of the software is released.

Select a Chapter

In addition to general tools, you are likely to find a few discipline-specific tools. The chapter selector is the doorway to the meat of the CW site. All of the tools described up to this point are general and present in all CW sites, but the resources you'll find within each chapter of the CW will match the topic and intent of the chapters in your textbook. This aspect of the CW is organized in parallel to the textbook. Notice that you can navigate anywhere in the CW with the navigation bar on the left side of the CW window. This vertical bar also lists all of the tools that are available to you within the chapter. As you may have discovered in reviewing the Help tool, all aspects of the CW are thoroughly described there. We encourage you to review the different tool descriptions and to play around with each in the chapter area of your CW. Each of the tools that you'll encounter within a chapter is designed to help you understand the topics presented in the chapter.

We would like to make a special note of the Feedback feature. The Internet is a dynamic place. It is not just different every day but also every second of every day. If you find something that you think will be helpful to others taking this course, that you feel is a mistake, or that could improve any of the CW sites, please send in feedback and the site will improve for everyone.

For a limited time following the purchase of a text you usually have access to technical support from the developing company. This resource can provide valuable information for technical problems that might surface. The e-mail, **web_tech_support@prenhall.com** will direct you to a support staff that will try to answer questions within a 24-hour period. In the current software environment, it is virtually impossible to develop highly interactive materials that will run flawlessly on all browsers but most material will work with Microsoft and Netscape browsers. Ask for help if you need it.

Navigation

In order to move through a Companion Website effectively, you should use the navigation bar in the left frame of the browser window. The top of the navigation bar offers controls for moving to the previous chapter, the next chapter, or to the top of the site (the index page).

The middle of the navigation bar provides links directly to the quiz, research, and communication modules. Sometimes this area will also include links to individual modules that have been gathered into groups. Various modules might include, multiple choice, true/false, essay, fill in the blank, and matching questions as well as objectives and web links.

The bottom portion of the navigation bar contains links to the Help files, User Profile, Feedback, Site Search, and Course Syllabus, if available.

Appendix B

Documenting Your Electronic Sources

Copyright laws came into effect when people started realizing that income could be made by selling their words. In an era dubbed "The Age of Information," knowledge and words are taking on more significance than ever. Laws requiring writers to *document* or give credit to the sources of their information, while evolving, are still in effect.

Various organizations have developed style manuals detailing, among other style matters, how to document sources in their particular disciplines. For writing in English composition and literature, Modern Language Association (MLA) and American Psychological Assocation (APA) guidelines are the most commonly used, but others such as those in *The Chicago Manual of Style* (CMS), are available. Always find out from your instructor what style to use in a specific assignment so that you can follow the appropriate guidelines.

For general information on MLA and APA citations, the best print sources are:

Gibaldi, Joseph. <u>MLA Handbook for Writers of Research Papers</u>. 4th ed. NY: MLA, 1995.

American Psychological Association. <u>Publication Manual of the American Psychological Association</u>. 4th ed. Washington: APA, 1994.

Because the methods of obtaining electronic information are developing so rapidly, printed style manuals have had difficulty in keeping up with the changes and in developing documentation styles for electronic sources. As a result, the most up-to-date information from the MLA and the APA about documenting online sources with URLs can be found on these organizations' websites. This Appendix shows you how to credit your electronic sources based on the information there.

When you cite electronic sources, it is vital to type every letter, number, symbol, and space accurately. Any error makes it impossible to retrieve your source. Since electronic sources tend to be transitory, printing a hard copy of your sources will make it easier for you to cite accurately and provide evidence for your documentation. MLA style encloses Internet addresses and URLs (Uniform Resource Locators) in angle brackets < >. If you see them around an address, do not use them as part of the address when you attempt to retrieve the source. APA style does not enclose URLs.

Modern Language Association (MLA) Style Guidelines

These guidelines follow the documentation style authorized by the Modern Language Association for electronic sources. Web sources are documented in basically the same way as traditional sources. According to the MLA website, the following items should be included if they are available:

1. Name of the author, editor, compiler, or translator of the source (if available and relevant), reversed for alphabetizing and followed by an abbreviation, such as *ed.*, if appropriate
2. Title of a poem, short story, article, or similar short work within a scholarly project, database, or periodical (in quotation marks); or title of a posting to a discussion list or forum (taken from the subject line and put in quotation marks), followed by the description *Online posting*
3. Title of a book (underlined)
4. Name of the editor, compiler, or translator of the text (if relevant and if not cited earlier), preceded by the appropriate abbreviation, such as *ed.*
5. Publication information for any print version of the source
6. Title of the scholarly project, database, periodical, or professional or personal site (underlined); or, for a professional or personal site with no title, a description such as *Home page*
7. Name of the editor of the scholarly project or database (if available)
8. Version number of the source (if not part of the title) or, for a journal, the volume number, issue number, or other identifying number
9. Date of electronic publication, of the latest update, or of posting
10. For a posting to a discussion list or forum, the name of the list or forum
11. The number range or total number of pages, paragraphs, or other sections, if they are numbered
12. Name of any institution or organization sponsoring or associated with the website
13. Date when the researcher accessed the source
14. Electronic address, or URL, of the source (in angle brackets)

From the Modern Language Association (MLA) <http://www.mla.org/main.stl.htm>.

Examples:

Book

Shaw, Bernard. <u>Pygmalion</u>. 1912. Bartleby Archive. 6 Mar. 1998
    <http://www.columbia.edu/acis/bartleby/shaw/>.

Poem

Carroll, Lewis. "Jabberwocky." 1872. 6 Mar. 1998.
    <http://www.jabberwocky.com/carroll/jabber/jabberwocky.html>.

Article in a Journal

Rehberger, Dean. "The Censoring of Project #17: Hypertext Bodies and
    Censorship." <u>Kairos</u> 2.2 (Fall 1997): 14 secs. 6 Mar. 1998
    <http://english.ttu.edu/kairos/2.2/index_f.html>.

Article in a Magazine

Viagas, Robert, and David Lefkowitz. "<u>Capeman</u> Closing Mar. 28."
    <u>Playbill</u> 5 Mar. 1998. 6 Mar. 1998 <http://www1.playbill.com/
    cgi-bin/plb/news?cmd=show&code=30763>.

Posting to a Discussion List

Grumman, Bob. "Shakespeare's Literacy." Online posting. 6 Mar. 1998.
    Deja News. <humanities.lit.author>.

Scholarly Project

<u>Voice of the Shuttle: Web Page for Humanities Research</u>. Ed. Alan Liu.
    Mar. 1998. U of California Santa Barbara. 8 Mar. 1998
    <http://humanitas.ucsb.edu/>.

Professional Site

<u>The Nobel Foundation Official Website</u>. The Nobel Foundation. 28 Feb.
    1998 <http://www.nobel.se/>.

Personal Site

Thiroux, Emily. Home page. 7 Mar. 1998
    <http://academic.csubak.edu/home/acadpro/departments/english/
    engthrx.htmlx>.

Synchronous Communications (such as MOOs, MUDs, and IRCs)

Ghostly Presence. Group Discussion. telnet 16 Mar. 1997
    <moo.du.org:8000/80anon/anonview/1 4036#focus>.

Gopher Sites

Banks, Vickie, and Joe Byers. "EDTECH." 18 Mar. 1997
    <gopher://ericyr.syr.edu:70/00/Listservs/EDTECH/README>.

FTP (File Transfer Protocol) Sites

```
U.S. Supreme Court directory. 6 Mar. 1998 <ftp://ftp.cwru.edu/
    U.S.Supreme.Court/>.
```

Synchronous communication

```
Author's last name, First name. Identifying label. "Title of
    work." xx Month 19xx. Name of forum. xx Month 19xx.
    <Telnet://lingua.networkname>.
```

Generally follow the guidelines for other on-line citations, modifying them wherever necessary, but always provide as much information as possible. Some cited material will require identifying labels (e.g., *Interview* or *Online posting*), but such labels should be neither underlined nor set within quotation marks. When documenting synchronous communications that are posted in MOO (multiuser domain, object oriented) and MUD (multiuser domain) forums, name the speaker or speakers; describe the event; provide the date of the event and the name of the forum (e.g., linguaMOO); and cite the date of access as well as the network name (including the prefix *Telnet://*).

Work From an Online Service

```
Author's last name, First name. Publication. 19xx. Internet Provider
    name. xx Month 19xx. Keyword: Name.
```

Or

```
Last name, First name. Publication. 19xx. Internet Provider name. xx
    Month 19xx. Path: Name; Name; Name.
```

```
Brash, Stephen B. "Bioprospecting the Public Domain." Cultural
    Anthropology 14.4 (1999): 535–56. ProQuest Direct. Teaneck Public
    Library, Teaneck, NJ. 7 Dec. 1999 <http://proquest.umi.com>.
```

Or

```
Dutton, Gail. "Greener Pigs." Popular Science 255.5 (1999): 38–39.
    ProQuest Direct. Teaneck Public Library, Teaneck, NJ. 7 Dec. 1999
    <http://proquest.umi.com>.
```

For works that have been accessed through an online service, either through a library service (e.g., ProQuest Direct or Lexis-Nexis) or through one of the large Internet providers (e.g., America Online), you may not know the URL of the source. In such cases, cite the keyword or path that led to the source, if applicable, and separate each individual item in the path with a semicolon; the keyword or path will be the last item in the citation. For sources accessed through library services, as above, cite the name of the service, the name of the library, the date you assessed the material, and the URL of the service's home page. If you also know the name of the database used, include that information (underlined) before the name of the on-line service.

American Psychological Association (APA) Style Guidelines

The most recent (4th) edition of the *Publication Manual of the American Psychological Association* includes general guidelines for citing electronic sources, and the APA has published specific examples for documenting Web sources on its Web page. Go to:

http://www.apa.org/journals/webref.html

In general, document these sources as you do traditional sources, giving credit to the author and including the title and date of publication. Include as much information as possible to help your reader to be able to retrieve the information. Any sources that are not generally available to your readers should be documented within the body of your writing as a personal communication but not included in your reference list. Such sources include material from listservs, newsgroups, Internet relay chats (IRCs), MOOs, MUDs, and e-mail.

According to information at the website for the American Psychological Association entitled "How to Cite Information From the World Wide Web"*

> All references begin with the same information that would be provided for a printed source (or as much of that information as possible). The Web information is then placed at the end of the reference. It is important to use the "Retrieved from" and the date because documents on the Web may change in content, move, or be removed from a site altogether. ... To cite a website in text (but not a specific document), it's sufficient to give the address (e.g., http://www.apa.org) there. No reference entry is needed.

Use the following guidelines to include a source in your reference list:

```
Name of author [if given]. (Publication date) [in parentheses]. Title
    of the article [following APA guidelines for capitalization].
    Title of periodical or electronic text [underlined]. Volume
    number and/or pages [if any]. Retrieved [include the date here]
    from the World Wide Web: [include the URL here, and do not end
    with a period]
```

*http://www.apa.org/journals/webref.html

Examples:

Journal Article

Fine, M. A. & Kurdek, L. A. (1993, November). Reflections
    on determining authorship credit and authorship order on
    faculty-student collaborations. American Psychologist, 48.11,
    1141-1147. Retrieved March 6, 1998 from the World Wide Web:
    http://www.apa.org/journals/amp/kurdek.html

Newspaper Article

Murray, B. (1998, February). Email bonding with your students. APA
    Monitor [Newspaper, selected stories on line]. Retrieved March 6,
    1998 from the World Wide Web: http://www.apa.org/monitor/bond.html

Appendix C

Glossary

Access Provider   A company that provides access to the Internet or a private network for a fee. (See Internet Service Provider.)

Agent   A type of software program that can be directed to automatically search the Internet or perform a specific function on behalf of a user. Spiders and worms, which roam the Internet, are the most common types of agents.

Anchor   An HTML tag used by a Web page author to designate a connection between a word in the text and a link to another page. (See HTML, Tag, and Link.)

AVI   This stands for Audio/Video Interleaved. It is a Microsoft Corporation format for encoding video and audio for digital transmission.

Backbone   The main network cable or link in a large internet.

Bandwidth   The capacity of a network line to carry user requests. Network lines such as a T1 are larger (have a higher bandwidth) and can carry more information than a lower bandwidth line such as an ISDN or a modem connection. (See ISDN and Modem.)

Bookmark   A list of URLs saved within a browser. The user can edit and modify the bookmark list to add and delete URLs as the user's interests change. Bookmark is a term used by Netscape to refer to the user's list of URLs; Hotlist is used by Mosaic for the same purpose. (See Hotlist and URL.)

Browser   A software program that is used to view and browse information on the Internet. Browsers are also referred to as clients. (See Client.)

Bulletin Board Service (BBS)   An electronic bulletin board, it is sometimes referred to as a BBS. Information on a BBS is posted to a computer where people can access, read, and comment on it. A BBS may or may not be connected to the Internet. Some are accessible by modem dial-in only.

Cache   A section of memory set aside to store information that is commonly used by the computer or by an active piece of software. Most browsers will create a cache for commonly-accessed images. An example might be the images that are common to the user's homepage. Retrieving images from the cache is much quicker than downloading the images from the original source each time they are required.

Chat room   A site that allows real-time person-to-person interactions.

Client   A software program used to view information from remote computers. Clients function in a Client-Server information exchange model. This term may also be loosely applied to the computer that is used to request information from the server. (See Server.)

Computer Virus   A program designed to infect a computer and possibly cause problems within the infected system. Viruses are typically passed from user to user through the exchange of an infected file. Numerous virus checkers or scanners are available to help you identify and inoculate your system against viruses.

Compressed file   A file or document that has been compacted to save memory space so that it can be easily and quickly transferred through the Internet.

Cookie   A small piece of information given temporarily to your Web browser by a Web server. The cookie is used to record information about you or your browsing behavior for later use by the server. For example, when you visit an online bookstore, a cookie will probably be passed to your browser to record book selections you make for purchase.

Cyberspace   This refers to the "world" of computers. It was coined by William Gibson in the novel *Neuromancer*.

Dial-Up Account   This refers to having registered permission to access a remote computer by which you are allowed to connect through a modem.

Domain   One of the different subsets of the Internet. The suffix found on the host name of an Internet server defines its domain. For example, the host name for Prentice Hall, the publisher of this book, is www.prenhall.com. The last part, .COM, indicates that Prentice Hall is a part of the commercial domain. Other domains include .MIL for military, .EDU for education, .ORG for non-profit organizations, .GOV for government organizations, and many more.

Download   The process of transferring a file, document, or program from a remote computer to a local computer. (See Upload.)

E-mail   The short name for electronic mail. E-mail is sent electronically from one person to another. Some companies have e-mail systems that are not part of the Internet. E-mail can be sent to one person or to many different people.

Encryption   A security procedure of coding information to prevent unwanted viewing. Information sent across a computer network is typically disassembled, shipped, and reassembled on the receiving computer. Encrypted information must be decrypted with a special "encryption key" by the receiving party.

Executable File   A file or program that can run (execute) by itself and that does not require another program. Some files, such as word processor documents, require an applications program for viewing them.

External Viewer Application   Browsers are software applications that enable users to display content distributed on the Web. Web information must be in one of a few specific formats before the browser can display it for the users. An External Viewer Application can be used to view files sent across the Web that cannot be viewed within the browser. These applications are said to be external because they do not operate within the browser. (See Plugin.)

FAQ   This stands for frequently asked questions. A FAQ is a file or document where a moderator or administrator will post commonly asked questions and their answers. Although it is very easy to communicate across the Internet, if you have a question, you should check for the answer in a FAQ first.

Firewall   A firewall is a network server that functions to control traffic flow between two separate networks. They are typically used to separate large government and corporate sites from the Internet. Some colleges use firewalls to protect certain areas of their network.

Flame   Degrading a person over the Internet is referred to as flaming. Nonverbal communication is not typically possible across a computer network, unless you have a video hookup, so misunderstandings often result. Anonymity of the flamer also contributes to such an exchange because people are more likely to make impolite statements given their physical separation.

FTP   This stands for File Transfer Protocol. It is a procedure used to transfer large files and programs from one computer to another. Access to the computer to transfer files may or may not require a password. Some FTP servers are set up to allow public access by anonymous log-on. This process is referred to as Anonymous FTP.

GIF   This stands for Graphics Interchange Format. It is a format created by CompuServe to allow electronic transfer of digital images. GIF files are a commonly-used format and can be viewed by both Mac and Windows users.

Gopher   A format structure and resource for providing information on the Internet. It was created at the University of Minnesota.

GUI   An acronym for Graphical User Interface. Macintosh and Windows operating systems are examples of typical GUIs.

Helper   This is software that is used to help a browser view information formats that it couldn't normally view.

Hits   This refers to a download request made by a browser to a server. Each file from a Web site that is requested by the browser is referred to as a hit. A Web page may be composed of numerous file elements and although hit counts are often reported as a measure of popularity, they can be misleading.

Homepage   In its specific sense, this refers to a Web document that a browser loads as its central navigational point to browse the Internet. It may also be used to refer to as Web page describing an individual. In the most general sense, it is used to refer to any Web document.

Host   Another name for a server computer. (See Server.)

Hotlist   This is a list of URLs saved within the Mosaic Web browser. This same list is referred to as a Bookmark within the Netscape Web browser.

HTML   This is an abbreviation for HyperText Markup Language, the common language used to write documents that appear on the World Wide Web.

HTTP   An abbreviation for HyperText Transport Protocol, the common protocol used to communicate between World Wide Web servers.

Hypertext   An embedded connection within a Web page that connects to a site within the viewed Web page or to a different Web page. Web pages use hypertext links to call up documents, images, sounds, and video files. The term hyperlink is a general term that applies to elements on Web pages other than text elements.

Icon   This refers to a visual representation of a file or program as it is represented on a typical windows graphic user interface (GUI). For example, Apple uses a trashcan icon to represent the place to put files you want to delete or remove from your computer. Microsoft uses a wastepaper basket.

Internet Relay Chat (IRC)   IRC is a network attached to the Internet. It allows users to converse in real time with other individuals. It is not typically a one-on-one conversation. Chat "rooms" are typically a very confusing place for beginners.

Internet Service Provider (ISP)   A company that provides Internet access is an ISP. Your ISP might be your school or a company to which you subscribe on a monthly basis.

Intranet   This refers to a network of networks that does not have a connection to THE Internet.

ISDN This stands for Integrated Services Digital Network. It is a digital phone line. ISDN service is typically more expensive but also offers customers added features such as a greater bandwidth. (See Bandwidth.)

Java An object-oriented programming language developed by Sun Microsystems.

JavaScript A scripting language developed by Netscape in cooperation with Sun Microsystems to add functionality to the basic Web page. It is not as powerful as Java and works primarily from the client side.

JPEG This stands for Joint Photographic Experts Group. It is one of the common standards for pictures on the Internet.

Local Area Network (LAN) A LAN is a small or local network, typically within a single building.

Link A text element or graphic within a document that has an embedded connection to another item. Web pages use links to access documents, images, sounds, and video files from the Internet, other documents on the local Web server, or other content on the Web page. Hyperlink is another name for link.

List Administrator An individual that monitors or oversees a mailing list. (See Mailing List.)

Login Generally, this refers to the act of connecting to a network but it may also indicate the need to enter a username or password to access a network or server.

Lurker An individual who connects to a chat room, bulletin board, or newsgroup and observes the conversation but does not participate.

Mailing List A functional group of e-mail addresses intended for making group mailings. It is used as a simple bulletin board. Some mailing lists are moderated by an individual and some are automatic. The most common mistake made by people using mailing lists is that they reply to a message and forget that everyone on the list will receive and potentially read their note. This can have embarrassing consequences.

MIME Type This stands for Multipurpose Internet Mail Extension. It is a standard used to identify files by their extension or suffix. Applications, like your e-mail client, are said to be MIME compliant when they can decode MIME suffixes. (See MOV, MPG, PDF.)

Mirror site Some sites on the Internet are very popular and under heavy demand by the viewing public and are potentially overloaded with traffic. Mirror sites are exact copies of the original site that help to distribute the traffic load, increasing efficiencies in delivering information.

Modem   A modem is a device used to send and receive information across a phone line by your computer. Computers speak digital and telephones speak analog. Essentially, a modem is a translator. Modems are only one kind of device available for connecting your computer to the outside world. Two other methods becoming more common for home use are ISDN and cable.

MOV   This stands for movie. It is a file extension for animations and videos in the QuickTime file format.

MPG/MPEG   This stands for Motion Picture Experts Group. It is a format for both digital audio and digital video files.

Multimedia   As a general definition, multimedia is the presentation of information by multiple media formats, such as words, images, and sound. Today, it's more commonly used to refer to presentations that use a lot of computer technology.

Nettiquette   This is a word created to mean Network Etiquette. It is a general list of practices and suggestions to help preserve the peace on the Internet. (See Flame.)

Newsgroup   This is the name for the discussion groups that can be on the *Usenet*. Not all newsgroups are accessible through the Internet. Some are accessible only through a modem connection. (See *Usenet*.)

Pathname   A convention for describing or outlining the location of a file or directory on a host computer. A URL is typically composed of several elements in addition to the pathname. For example, in this URL: http://www.prenhall.com/pubguide/index.html, http:// describes the protocol for a Web server, www.prenhall.com is the name of the host or server, /pubguide/ is the pathname, and index.html is the file name.

PDF   This stands for Portable Document Format. It is a file format that allows authors to distribute formatted, high-resolution documents across the Internet. A free viewer, Adobe Acrobat Reader, is required to view PDF documents.

Plug-in   This is a resource or program that can be added to a browser to extend its function and capabilities.

QuickTime (QT)   A file format developed by Apple Computer so that computers can play digital audio, animation, and video files. (See MOV, MPG.)

Robot   An automated program used to search and explore the Internet. Some popular search engines use these programs.

Search Engine   An online service or utility that enables users to query and search the Internet for user-defined information. They are typically free services to the user. (See Robot.)

Search String   A logical collection of terms or phrases used to describe a search request. Some search engines enable the user to define strings with Boolean cues such as AND, NOT, or OR. (See Search Engine.)

Server   A software program used to provide, or serve, information to remote computers. Servers function in a Client-Server information exchange model. This term may also be loosely applied to the computer that is used to serve the information. (See Client.)

Shareware   Software that is provided to the public on a try-before-you-buy basis. Shareware functions on the honor system. Once you've used it for a while, you are expected to pay a small fee. Two similar varieties of software are Freeware and Postcardware. Freeware is just that, free for your use and the owners of Post-cardware simply ask you to send them a postcard to thank them for the product.

Shockwave   Shockwave is a plugin that allows Macromedia programs to be played on your Web browser. Many learning tools are beginning to be posted to the Web as Shockwave files. Visit Macromedia's Web site for more information and to download the plug-in (http://www.macromedia.com/). (See Plug-in.)

Signature   A signature is text that is automatically added to the bottom of electronic communications such as e-mail or newsgroup postings. A signature usually lists the name and general information about the person making the posting. Using a signature means that you don't have to repeatedly type your name and return information every time you send a note.

SPAM   The electronic version of junk mail. It also refers to the behavior of sending or posting a single note to numerous e-mail or newsgroup accounts. It is considered to be very bad nettiquette.

Stuff   The action of compressing a file using the Stuff-It program. This is a Macintosh format.

Table   A specific formatting element found in HTML pages. Tables are used on HTML documents to visually organize information.

Telnet   The process of remotely connecting and using a computer at a distant location.

Thread   This describes a linked series of newsgroup postings. It represents a conversation stream. Messages posted on active newsgroups are likely to spur numerous replies each of which can spin off into an independent conversation. The nature of newsgroups allows a reader to move forward or backward through a conversation as if moving along a string or thread.

Topic Drift   This describes the phenomena observed in many on-line conversations, typically chat or newsgroup, where the topic will drift or change from the original posting.

Upload   The process of moving or transferring a document, file, or program from one computer to another computer.

URL   An abbreviation for Universal Resource Locator. In its basic sense, it is an address used by people on the Internet to locate documents. URLs have a common format that describes the protocol for information transfer, the host computer address, the path to the desired file, and the name of the file requested.

Usenet   A worldwide system of discussion groups, also called newsgroups. There are many thousands of newsgroups, but only some of these are accessible from the Internet.

User Name   An ID used as identification on a computer or network. It is a string of alphanumeric characters that may or may not have any resemblance to a user's real name.

Viewer   A program used to view data files within or outside a browser. (See External Viewer Application.)

Virtual Reality (VR)   A simulation of three-dimensional space on the computer. (See VRML.)

VRML   This stands for Virtual Reality Markup Language. It was developed to allow the creation of virtual reality worlds. Your browser may need a specific plug-in to view VRML pages.

WAV   This stands for Waveform sound format. It is a Microsoft Corporation format for encoding sound files.

Web (WWW)   This stands for the World Wide Web. When loosely applied, this term refers to the Internet and all of its associated incarnations, including Gopher, FTP, HTTP, and others. More specifically, this term refers to a subset of the servers on the Internet that use HTTP to transfer hyperlinked documents in a page-like format.

Webmaster   This is the general title given to the administrator of a Web server.

Web Page   A single file as viewed within a Web browser. Several Web pages linked together represent a website.